Growth Mindset

How to Release Your Hidden Potential

(A Powerful Analysis to Help You on the Road to Transforming Your Social Life)

Joseph Leeper

Published By **John Kembrey**

Joseph Leeper

All Rights Reserved

Growth Mindset: How to Release Your Hidden Potential (A Powerful Analysis to Help You on the Road to Transforming Your Social Life)

ISBN 978-1-7777614-7-9

No part of this guidebook shall be reproduced in any form without permission in writing from the publisher except in the case of brief quotations embodied in critical articles or reviews.

Legal & Disclaimer

The information contained in this book is not designed to replace or take the place of any form of medicine or professional medical advice. The information in this book has been provided for educational & entertainment purposes only.

The information contained in this book has been compiled from sources deemed reliable, and it is accurate to the best of the Author's knowledge; however, the Author cannot guarantee its accuracy and validity and cannot be held liable for any errors or omissions. Changes are periodically made to this book. You must consult your doctor or get professional medical advice before using any of the suggested remedies, techniques, or information in this book.

Upon using the information contained in this book, you agree to hold harmless the Author from and against any damages, costs, and expenses, including any legal fees potentially resulting from the application of any of the information provided by this guide. This disclaimer applies to any damages or injury caused by the use and application, whether directly or indirectly, of any advice or information presented, whether for breach of contract, tort, negligence, personal injury, criminal intent, or under any other cause of action.

You agree to accept all risks of using the information presented inside this book. You need to consult a professional medical practitioner in order to ensure you are both able and healthy enough to participate in this program.

Table Of Contents

Chapter 1: Understanding Fixed Mindsets 1

Chapter 2: Strategies For Overcoming Obstacles 7

Chapter 3: Applying A Growth Mindset In Daily Life 29

Chapter 4: Case Studies And Real-Life Examples................................. 49

Chapter 5: Cultivating A Growth Mindset In Others................................. 79

Chapter 6: What's Mindset? 109

Chapter 7: Why Is Mindset Important? 117

Chapter 8: Fixed Vs Growth Mindset ... 126

Chapter 9: The Dangers Of A Fixed Mindset 135

Chapter 10: The Power Of A Growth Mindset 144

Chapter 11: Can You Change Your Mindset?................................. 154

Chapter 12: Strategies To Develop A Growth Mindset.................................. 165

Chapter 13: Dealing With Setbacks 175

Chapter 1: Understanding Fixed Mindsets

To virtually recognize the idea of a Growth Mindset, it is vital to assessment it with its counterpart: the Fixed Mindset. Understanding the variations amongst these mindsets is a critical foundation in your journey to private and expert development.

1. The Fixed Mindset:

A Fixed Mindset is a notion machine in which people perceive their capabilities and intelligence as innate and unchanging. In specific phrases, they accept as true with that you are born with a tremendous stage of intelligence, talent, and character inclinations, and people traits live surprisingly static for the duration of existence. People with a Fixed Mindset often see effort as fruitless, as they recollect that inherent abilties decide success.

2. The Growth Mindset:

Conversely, a Growth Mindset is the perception that skills and intelligence can be superior and stepped forward over time. Those with a Growth Mindset view try and mastering due to the fact the course to mastery. They embody stressful situations, look at from failures, and accept as authentic with that setbacks are stepping stones toward success. In a Growth Mindset, individuals see their capacity as malleable and their potential to change and develop as countless.

To illustrate the versions most of the ones mindsets, keep in thoughts the following situations:

Challenges: When faced with a tough assignment, someone with a Fixed Mindset can also avoid it, fearing failure, whilst someone with a Growth Mindset might also want to technique it as an opportunity to look at and decorate.

Failures: A person with a Fixed Mindset should probable view a setback as evidence in their loss of capacity, main to self-doubt. In contrast, a person with a Growth Mindset would possibly see failure as a risk to enlarge new strategies and skills, developing their willpower to try another time.

Effort: Those with a Fixed Mindset will be inclined to pull away from exerting attempt, as they take delivery of as proper with expertise by myself have to bring about fulfillment. In assessment, individuals with a Growth Mindset include strive as a method to accumulate their desires.

This vital assessment among Fixed and Growth Mindsets shapes our attitudes, behaviors, and ultimately, our effects in severa elements of life. Recognizing which mindset you presently preserve is step one closer to shifting your mind-set and reaping the advantages of a Growth Mindset. In the chapters in advance, we're capable of find out strategies that will help you make this variation and begin to cope with life's limitations with renewed power and resilience.

The Science Behind the Growth Mindset

The Growth Mindset is not handiest a philosophical concept; it is firmly rooted in intellectual research and cognitive generation. Understanding the medical foundations of the Growth Mindset can provide a boost on your conviction in its effectiveness and provide belief into why it honestly works. In this bankruptcy, we are able to discover some key medical findings that underpin the Growth Mindset.

1. Brain Plasticity:

One of the applicable tenets of the Growth Mindset is the concept that our talents can be advanced through strive and studying. This belief is supported thru the idea of neuroplasticity, this is the thoughts's functionality to reorganize itself, shape new neural connections, and adapt all through existence. Neuroscience studies has mounted that the thoughts can exchange in response to revel in and training. This method that with exercise and reading, we're capable of physical exchange our thoughts's shape and, consequently, our abilities.

2. Mindset and Effort:

Psychologist Carol Dweck's awesome research at the Growth Mindset has observed out that humans with a Growth Mindset are much more likely to include try and persist in the face of disturbing situations. Dweck's research display that humans with a Growth Mindset usually have a tendency to have a greater fine reaction to attempt because they see it as a manner to beautify their skills. This no longer extraordinary affects their regular overall performance however moreover their elegant mind-set in the direction of learning and success.

three. Impact on Learning and Achievement:

Studies inside the concern of education have tested that students who're taught approximately the Growth Mindset usually have a tendency to perform higher academically. They turn out to be extra inspired, resilient, and open to learning. Moreover, they will be a whole lot lots much less probable to be discouraged by way of manner of way of setbacks and are more likely to see challenges as opportunities to develop.

4. Emotional Resilience:

Research has additionally indicated that humans with a Growth Mindset normally tend to experience extra emotional resilience. They are better organized to cope with strain, anxiety, and setbacks due to the reality they view such tales as possibilities for increase in region of as threats to their conceitedness.

Chapter 2: Strategies For Overcoming Obstacles

Embracing a Growth Mindset is the first step in the route of overcoming limitations, however it's far the techniques you rent that truly make a distinction. In this chapter, we are able to delve into practical strategies and techniques for co nquering challenges, setbacks, and barriers for your life.

1. Embrace Challenges as Opportunities:

Reframe your mind-set on disturbing conditions. Instead of viewing them as threats, see them as opportunities for growth and learning. When you encounter a hard undertaking, remind your self that it's a threat to broaden new abilities and knowledge.

2. Persistence and the Role of Effort:

Understand that try is a essential issue of fulfillment. Recognize that patience is high to overcoming limitations. When you face a setback, don't give up; as an alternative, set up greater attempt and strive another time.

3. Learning from Failures and Setbacks:

Embrace your failures as precious studying reports. Analyze what went wrong, perceive the instructions you could draw from the setback, and use that records to evolve and enhance your technique.

4. Seeking and Utilizing Feedback:

Be open to positive comments from others. Feedback can offer insights into areas for improvement. Use comments as a device for private and expert increase, and do no longer apprehend it as grievance.

five. Resilience and Bouncing Back:

Build resilience to get higher from setbacks. Understand that resilience is the capability to face up to adversity and pop out stronger. It consists of coping mechanisms, strain manage, and a notion for your functionality to overcome issues.

6. Goal Setting and Motivation:

Set clean, potential goals that inspire you to paintings through boundaries. Well-described goals provide a experience of path and reason, preserving you centered and driven inside the face of demanding situations.

7. Developing Self-Belief:

Cultivate self-self assurance to your capability to test and adapt. Believe for your ability to overcome disturbing situations and prevail. Positive self-belief can be a effective motivator and deliver of resilience.

eight. Positive Self-Talk:

Monitor your inner speak. Replace self-limiting ideals and lousy self-communicate with amazing, growth-oriented language. Encourage yourself to maintain shifting forward and to view obstacles as possibilities for boom.

9. Visualization and Mental Preparation:

Use visualization strategies to mentally prepare for demanding conditions. Visualizing success can help reduce anxiety and collect self assurance, making it much less tough to deal with boundaries.

10. Time Management and Organization:

Effective time control and corporation will will let you navigate barriers greater efficiently. Structure your duties, set priorities, and allocate time for problem-solving and gaining knowledge of.

11. Seeking Support and Collaboration:

Don't hesitate to are searching for guide from buddies, mentors, or colleagues. Collaboration can offer smooth views and solutions to barriers that might be difficult to address by myself.

12. Adaptability and Flexibility:

Be open to alternate and inclined to comply your techniques as wished. Recognize that the direction to fulfillment is not often linear, and versatility is high to overcoming surprising obstacles.

These strategies, even as mixed with a Growth Mindset, offer a powerful toolkit for confronting and conquering limitations in various factors of your existence. Whether you are going through demanding situations in your schooling, profession, relationships, or non-public development, those strategies allow you to navigate and conquer them with resilience and resolution.

Embracing Challenges as Opportunities

One of the crucial standards of the Growth Mindset is the capability to view disturbing situations as opportunities for non-public and professional increase. Embracing stressful conditions with this attitude can redesign the manner you technique issues and setbacks. In this section, we're going to find out strategies for embracing traumatic situations as possibilities:

1. Reframe Your Perspective:

Start thru reframing your angle on annoying situations. Instead of viewing them as daunting limitations, see them as probabilities to analyze and enhance. Recognize that demanding situations are the crucible where your talents are tested and subtle.

2. Embrace a Learning Attitude:

Adopt a getting to know mind-set towards challenges. Understand that each project offers a lesson. Approach every trouble with the interest and exuberance of a pupil, eager to advantage new insights and capabilities.

three. Set Growth-Oriented Goals:

When faced with a project, set growth-oriented desires. Define what you need to observe or advantage thru the experience. Having clean dreams can offer path and motivation as you deal with the venture.

4. Break Challenges into Smaller Steps:

Sometimes, demanding situations can seem overwhelming. To make them greater conceivable, damage them into smaller, greater digestible steps. Each step you triumph over brings you in the direction of the general reason.

5. Practice Positive Self-Talk:

Monitor yourself-talk whilst dealing with annoying situations. Replace lousy, self-proscribing mind with first-class and boom-oriented language. Remind your self of your skills and recognition on answers, not problems.

6. Focus on Effort, Not Just Outcomes:

Shift your hobby from the give up result to the try you install. Understand that success is usually a result of difficult art work and staying strength. Celebrate your dedication and development, regardless of the instant final results.

7. Accept That Mistakes Are Part of Learning:

Understand that making errors is a natural part of the mastering technique. When you come upon setbacks, see them as stepping stones inside the course of development.

Reflect for your errors, examine from them, and follow those commands transferring in advance.

8. Seek Challenges Proactively:

Don't expect annoying conditions to return to you; are looking for them out proactively. By stepping from your comfort region and intentionally taking over new annoying conditions, you could boost up your personal growth.

9. Celebrate Effort and Progress:

Acknowledge and characteristic a laugh your try and improvement throughout your journey. Recognize the stairs you have got were given taken, the information you've got were given obtained, and the skills you've got were given advanced alongside the manner.

10. Learn from Others:

Seek concept and steerage from individuals who have faced comparable traumatic conditions. Learn from their research, strategies, and the knowledge they could provide.

11. Maintain a Growth Mindset Circle:

Surround your self with those who additionally embody stressful situations as possibilities. Your social circle can extensively have an effect in your attitude. Connect with individuals who encourage your increase and resilience.

Persistence and the Role of Effort

In the context of overcoming barriers with a Growth Mindset, endurance and the position of try are paramount. These factors are the the use of forces that let you tackle demanding conditions, setbacks, and hurdles. Here's a better observe how they make a contribution to your fulfillment:

1. Recognizing the Importance of Persistence:

Persistence is the unwavering dedication to maintain shifting in advance no matter limitations and setbacks. It's the willingness to undergo troubles and setbacks in the pursuit of your goals. Understand that patience is a key detail in conducting long-time period achievement.

2. The Connection Between Effort and Achievement:

The Growth Mindset emphasizes that fulfillment is a stop result of effort, gaining knowledge of, and boom, not innate expertise. It teaches that, with strive, you may triumph over any undertaking and acquire your desires. This perception inside the hyperlink amongst strive and fulfillment is a middle principle of the Growth Mindset.

three. Embrace Effort as a Path to Mastery:

Instead of fearing strive or seeing it as a burden, embody it as a direction to mastery. Effort is the approach thru that you improve and expand your skills. When you install strive, you're actively making an funding for your non-public and professional growth.

four. Learn from the Process:

While the give up reason is essential, take into account that the journey, and the strive you make investments along the manner, are simply as valuable. Learning from the manner, the mistakes you are making, and the try you put in is crucial for non-public boom and improvement.

5. Persistence in the Face of Setbacks:

When you encounter setbacks or disasters, do not allow them to discourage you. Instead, use these studies as possibilities to demonstrate your endurance. Understand that resilience and tenacity in the face of adversity can cause eventual success.

6. Goal Setting and Motivation:

Setting clean, viable dreams can offer motivation and path in your efforts. When you have got a goal in thoughts, it turns into lots less complicated to persist, as you understand what you're working in the direction of.

7. Celebrate Small Wins:

Recognize and characteristic fun your small achievements alongside the way. These victories, irrespective of how minor, are a testomony to your staying energy and attempt. Celebrating them can enhance your motivation to keep going.

eight. Self-Compassion:

Be type and compassionate to your self. Acknowledge that persistence may be challenging, and there can be instances whilst you want a damage. Self-compassion guarantees you do now not burn out and can hold your attempt over the long time.

nine. Seek Support and Guidance:

Don't hesitate to are seeking out aid and guidance from mentors, pals, or colleagues. They can provide encouragement and recommendation to help you hold your staying power, even within the face of problems.

10. Visualize Success:

Use visualization techniques to examine the a hit outcome of your efforts. Visualizing your desires can beef up your motivation and hold you continuously shifting in advance.

Persistence and attempt, on the identical time as blended with a Growth Mindset, create a effective machine for overcoming barriers. Recognize the rate of your tenacity and resolution, and recognize that with sustained attempt, you may conquer challenges and reap your aspirations.

Embracing annoying conditions as possibilities is a transformative attitude shift that empowers you to deal with life's hurdles with enthusiasm and a desire to analyze. By utilizing the ones techniques, you could foster a Growth Mindset and discover boom and achievement in even the maximum worrying situations.

Learning from Failures and Setbacks

Failures and setbacks are an inevitable part of lifestyles, however they can be effective stepping stones to boom and fulfillment even as approached with a Growth Mindset. Here are strategies for reading from disasters and setbacks:

1. Embrace a Positive Perspective:

Instead of viewing failures as defeats, see them as opportunities to analyze and decorate. Adopt a mindset that perceives setbacks as a herbal a part of the gaining knowledge of device.

2. Analyze the Failure:

Take time to mirror on what went wrong. What elements contributed to the setback? Was it because of a lack of strive, a wrong approach, or out of doors conditions? Gaining perception into the reasons of failure is the first step in learning from it.

three. Extract Lessons:

Identify the particular lessons you could draw from the failure. What did you find out approximately yourself, the project, or the approach you took? Every setback holds treasured statistics that can inform your destiny moves.

4. Adapt Your Approach:

Use the insights acquired from your assessment to evolve your method. Adjust your strategies, set new dreams, and make changes that can boom your possibilities of achievement inside the future.

five. Develop Resilience:

Building resilience is vital for bouncing back from setbacks. Recognize that worrying situations and disasters are part of the adventure. Develop coping mechanisms and pressure control techniques to navigate the ones moments effectively.

6. Set Realistic Expectations:

Ensure your dreams and expectancies are practical. Sometimes, disasters upward thrust up because we set not possible goals. Adjust your desires to align together together with your abilities and available belongings.

7. Maintain a Growth Mindset:

Reinforce your Growth Mindset whilst dealing with screw ups. Remember that your abilities may be superior thru strive and getting to know. Continue to accept as right with for your functionality to decorate and grow.

8. Seek Feedback:

Don't hesitate to are searching out comments from mentors, buddies, or experts inside the region. Constructive remarks can offer valuable insights and help you come to be privy to areas for development.

nine. Avoid Self-Blame:

While it's miles important to take obligation in your moves, avoid immoderate self-blame. Understand that setbacks regularly give up cease result from a combination of factors, now not completely your shortcomings.

10. Keep a Growth Journal:

Consider preserving a boom magazine in that you report your reports, collectively with disasters, training found out, and your development plans. This magazine can characteristic a valuable beneficial useful useful resource for tracking your boom.

eleven. Share Your Experience:

Sharing your reports with setbacks and what you've got were given observed cannot only help others but moreover beautify your information. Teaching what you have got learned from failure can solidify the ones instructions.

12. Stay Persistent:

Most importantly, do now not surrender. Keep moving forward, information that every failure is a step toward achievement. Persistence within the face of adversity is a hallmark of a Growth Mindset.

Learning from disasters and setbacks is an vital skill that may bring about personal and expert increase. When you method the ones critiques with a Growth Mindset and rent the ones strategies, you could remodel setbacks into treasured opportunities for self-improvement and achievement.

Seeking and Utilizing Feedback

Feedback is a precious beneficial useful resource for personal and expert growth. It offers insights, views, and steerage that help you to triumph over limitations and continually enhance. Here are strategies for correctly in search of and utilising remarks:

1. Recognize the Value of Feedback:

Understand that remarks is a present. It gives you with valuable statistics that permit you to select out regions for improvement and develop to your endeavors.

2. Create an Open Feedback Environment:

Foster an environment wherein comments is suggested and welcomed. Whether to your place of business, personal relationships, or academic settings, allow humans understand that their input is valued.

three. Seek Feedback Proactively:

Don't assume comments to come back to you. Actively are trying to find it out from friends, mentors, supervisors, or colleagues. Be unique for your requests, that specialize in areas you want to improve.

4. Be Open to Constructive Criticism:

Approach comments with an open and receptive attitude. Avoid becoming protecting or dismissive of grievance. Instead, see it as an opportunity to research and increase.

five. Ask for Specific Feedback:

When searching out feedback, ask for precise, actionable insights. For example, inquire about your typical overall performance on a particular undertaking, your communication competencies, or your hassle-solving skills.

6. Listen Actively:

When receiving remarks, pay interest attentively and without interruption. Show appreciation for the remarks and ask clarifying questions if critical to certainly recognize the factors being made.

7. Reflect on Feedback:

Take time to mirror on the feedback you get maintain of. Consider the manner it aligns with yourself-assessment and whether or not or now not it highlights areas wherein you could beautify.

eight. Distinguish Between Constructive and Destructive Feedback:

Not all remarks is similarly treasured. Learn to differentiate among optimistic feedback, which gives guidelines for improvement, and damaging remarks, which can be unhelpful or biased.

nine. Act on Feedback:

The proper price of comments is in your response to it. Identify actionable steps based at the remarks you've got got obtained, and actively artwork on implementing adjustments.

10. Set Goals for Improvement:

Use comments to set particular goals for personal or professional development. This ensures that you are actively the use of comments as a device for growth.

eleven. Continuous Feedback Loop:

Establish a non-stop feedback loop for your existence. Regularly are looking for, gather, and act on feedback, allowing it to turn out to be a normal a part of your increase journey.

12. Express Gratitude:

Always specific gratitude to individuals who provide you with remarks. Whether it is praise or optimistic criticism, allow them to apprehend that you respect their effort and time in helping you develop.

13. Provide Feedback to Others:

Be willing to reciprocate and provide remarks to others. Your insights and observations may be simply as precious to their growth as remarks is to yours.

Effectively seeking out and the usage of feedback is a capacity that allow you to overcome limitations and boost up your private and expert improvement. By growing an open remarks environment and actively incorporating feedback into your boom method, you may continuously refine your abilities and overcome demanding situations extra efficaciously.

Chapter 3: Applying A Growth Mindset In Daily Life

Incorporating a Growth Mindset into your everyday life can bring about personal and professional boom. Here are realistic strategies to use this mindset in your normal sports:

1. Embrace Challenges:

Seek out disturbing conditions on your private and professional lifestyles. View them as opportunities to take a look at and broaden in preference to as threats to your competence.

2. Persist within the Face of Setbacks:

When you encounter barriers, preserve your staying strength. Remember that attempt is a route to mastery, and setbacks are stepping stones to success.

3. Encourage Learning:

Cultivate a thirst for statistics. Approach every day as an possibility to investigate a few factor new, whether or not it is a talents, a chunk of records, or a life lesson.

four. Use Positive Self-Talk:

Monitor your internal communicate and update horrible self-communicate with exceptional affirmations that improve your belief in your functionality to enhance and develop.

5. Accept Constructive Feedback:

Welcome feedback from others as a treasured tool for self-development. Use it to comply, develop, and refine your skills.

6. Develop Resilience:

Practice resilience by the usage of viewing adversity as a threat to emerge as stronger. Use coping mechanisms to navigate disturbing conditions and preserve a effective outlook.

7. Set Meaningful Goals:

Set clean and great desires that inspire you and align together together along with your values. Regularly evaluate and adjust your desires to keep them applicable.

eight. Maintain a Balanced Perspective:

Keep a balanced angle whilst going via successes and failures. Understand that each are a part of the increase journey.

9. Seek Opportunities for Growth:

Actively are searching for out possibilities for non-public and professional development. This can involve pursuing new critiques, guides, or stressful conditions.

10. Mentor and Inspire Others:

Share your know-how and insights with others, and inspire them to increase a Growth Mindset. Mentoring and coaching can enhance your very own beliefs and growth.

eleven. Stay Curious:

Maintain a enjoy of hobby for your every day lifestyles. Ask questions, explore new pastimes, and method the arena with an open and inquisitive thoughts.

12. Overcome Procrastination:

Combat procrastination by using using manner of the use of time manipulate strategies, putting clean priorities, and breaking responsibilities into attainable steps.

13. Focus on the Process:

Shift your recognition from the result to the gadget itself. Enjoy the adventure of increase in region of really fixating at the vacation spot.

14. Reflect and Learn:

Regularly reflect to your reviews, each the high-quality and the hard ones. Extract commands from each scenario and take a look at them shifting in advance.

15. Celebrate Small Wins: moments are a testament to your boom.

sixteen. Maintain a Growth Circle:

Surround your self with individuals who also include a Growth Mindset. Your social circle may also have an impact on and beautify your thoughts-set.

Applying a Growth Mindset on your every day existence is a transformative exercising that would motive non-forestall self-improvement and an extended capability to triumph over boundaries and attain achievement. By constantly integrating these strategies, you can beautify your mind-set and navigate lifestyles's demanding situations with extra resilience and determination

The Impact of a Growth Mindset on Decision-Making

A Growth Mindset can significantly impact the way you approach selection-making, major to greater informed and resilient options. Here's how a Growth Mindset can effect choice-making:

1. Embracing Challenges and Risks:

Individuals with a Growth Mindset are more likely to consist of disturbing conditions and take calculated risks. They see demanding situations as possibilities to investigate and develop, and this thoughts-set can purpose them to make selections that contain stepping out of their consolation zones.

2. Persistence inside the Face of Failure:

Those with a Growth Mindset usually usually tend to persist within the face of failure. When a selection does now not yield the predicted very last consequences, they view it as a threat to research and alter. This resilience can bring about greater tenacious choice-making.

three. Willingness to Learn:

A Growth Mindset fosters a sturdy preference to research and adapt. This eagerness to research can cause choices that are based totally on a deeper data of the scenario and the willingness to gather new information or abilties as wanted.

four. Openness to Feedback:

Decision-makers with a Growth Mindset are greater open to feedback from others. They see feedback as a valuable useful resource for reinforcing their picks and are willing to adjust their options based totally on tremendous input.

five. Learning from Mistakes:

Individuals with a Growth Mindset are much more likely to view mistakes as a part of the reading approach. When alternatives cause mistakes, they see them as opportunities for personal and expert growth, which can cause higher selection-making in the destiny.

6. Goal-Oriented Decision-Making:

Those with a Growth Mindset often make choices that align with their desires and aspirations. They set goals and make selections that make a contribution to their personal and expert improvement.

7. Adaptability:

A Growth Mindset encourages adaptability in selection-making. When activities trade or sudden annoying conditions stand up, human beings with this thoughts-set are much more likely to modify their choices and strategies to house new information.

eight. Confidence in Problem-Solving:

A Growth Mindset can increase self assurance in a unmarried's problem-fixing capabilities. When faced with complex choices, individuals are much more likely to believe of their functionality to discover answers and technique them with a immoderate best mind-set.

9. Continuous Self-Improvement:

Decision-makers with a Growth Mindset are dedicated to non-stop self-development. They see their decisions as possibilities for growth and self-mirrored image, essential to a extra informed and powerful choice-making manner.

10. Focus on the Process:

A Growth Mindset shifts the point of interest from instantaneous consequences to the choice-making technique itself. This method encourages people to make selections which is probably well-reasoned and primarily based on the splendid to be had information.

In summary, a Growth Mindset has a profound impact on choice-making by way of the use of way of fostering resilience, adaptability, a determination to getting to know, and a focal point on non-public and expert growth. Individuals with this mind-set are much more likely to make informed choices that align with their long-term goals and are higher prepared to investigate from every fulfillment and failure.

Navigating Career Challenges with a Growth Mindset

Your career is packed with challenges, and a Growth Mindset may be a powerful device for navigating those obstacles. Here's a way to apply a Growth Mindset to conquer profession traumatic situations:

1. Embrace Change and Adaptability:

View adjustments to your career as possibilities for boom. Be adaptable and open to new testimonies, roles, and obligations.

2. Learn from Setbacks:

When you face setbacks or screw ups for your career, see them as chances to have a take a look at and enhance. Analyze what went incorrect, adapt your technique, and persevere.

3. Seek Feedback:

Actively searching for comments from supervisors, pals, and mentors. Use this remarks to perceive regions for development and refine your skills.

4. Set Career Goals: Establish clear and bold profession goals. Having described goals offers motivation and direction, helping you navigate demanding situations with cause.

five. Develop a Plan:

Create a career improvement plan outlining the steps and techniques required to obtain your dreams. Having a plan in vicinity makes it much less complex to tackle worrying situations.

6. Network and Build Relationships:

Cultivate a professional network that can provide assist and steering sooner or later of hard times. Networking also can open up new possibilities.

7. Take on New Challenges:

Volunteer for responsibilities and initiatives that take you out of your consolation zone. Embrace opportunities for boom and talent improvement.

eight. View Rejections as Opportunities:

If you face rejection or setbacks in your career, see them as possibilities to find out opportunity paths or to decorate your qualifications.

nine. Encourage Self-Improvement:

Commit to non-stop self-development and lifelong studying. This mindset positions you to evolve to the evolving desires of your industry.

10. Stay Positive and Resilient:

Maintain a excessive wonderful outlook and assemble resilience. Understand that resilience is the functionality to face up to career annoying situations and bounce back stronger.

eleven. Mentor and Seek Mentoring:

Mentor others to your discipline to boost your information and abilities. Additionally, are searching for mentoring from skilled specialists who can offer valuable insights.

12. Stay Informed:

Stay up to date with enterprise dispositions and modifications. Being nicely-informed will let you proactively navigate profession annoying conditions.

thirteen. Build Confidence:

Cultivate self-self perception in your profession skills. Believe in your potential to overcome stressful conditions and seize opportunities.

14. Celebrate Achievements:

Acknowledge and feature an amazing time your profession achievements, irrespective of how small. Recognizing your improvement can raise motivation and resilience.

15. Focus on Long-Term Growth:

Remember that your profession is a long-term adventure. Take a large-image angle and remember traumatic situations as part of your trendy growth.

sixteen. Use Failures to Fuel Success:

Instead of permitting screw ups to discourage you, use them as gas for achievement. Learn out of your mistakes and use that knowledge to make greater informed choices.

Applying a Growth Mindset in your career allow you to navigate annoying situations with resilience and determination. By embracing change, studying from opinions, and constantly improving, you'll be better organized to stand and overcome profession barriers.

Health and Wellness: Overcoming Obstacles

Maintaining correct health and well being often includes overcoming numerous limitations. A Growth Mindset can be a valuable device in addressing the ones worrying conditions. Here's a way to observe a Growth Mindset to navigate boundaries in the context of fitness and fitness:

1. View Health as a Journey:

See your fitness and wellness as an ongoing journey in place of a holiday spot. Understand that setbacks and barriers are natural factors of this adventure.

2. Embrace a Positive Perspective:

Maintain a extraordinary outlook for your fitness. Even even as facing fitness traumatic situations, awareness on what you may do to enhance in preference to living on limitations.

3. Set Realistic Goals:

Set capability health and well being goals which can be precise, measurable, and time-sure. These goals need to inspire you to do so with out overwhelming you.

four. Develop Healthy Habits:

Cultivate healthy behavior and carrying activities. Incorporate ordinary exercising, balanced vitamins, and adequate sleep into your each day lifestyles to sell regular well being.

five. Learn from Setbacks:

When you come upon setbacks to your health adventure, address them as possibilities to investigate and adapt. Analyze what went incorrect and make modifications.

6. Seek Support:

Don't hesitate to are searching for assist from healthcare professionals, therapists, or guide groups while wanted. These property can provide steerage and encouragement.

7. Maintain a Growth Mindset for Learning:

Approach health and health with a Growth Mindset. Understand that you may check and expand in this place, and that exchange is viable via strive and gaining knowledge of.

eight. Practice Resilience:

Build resilience within the face of health annoying situations. Understand that setbacks are transient and that you could leap again with perseverance and determination.

nine. Seek Education:

Educate your self approximately your fitness and nicely-being wishes. Knowledge empowers you to make knowledgeable picks and take proactive steps.

10. Monitor Progress:

Regularly song your development inside the route of health and health desires. This allows you stay caused and modify your strategies as desired.

eleven. Celebrate Small Wins:

Recognize and characteristic amusing your achievements in health and nicely being, irrespective of how minor. Each step within the direction of advanced health is a achievement well properly really worth acknowledging.

12. Stay Persistent:

Keep up the try even if development is slow or while you stumble upon barriers. Persistence is a key thing in achieving and maintaining accurate health.

13. Focus on Self-Care:

Prioritize self-care practices that make a contribution for your physical and intellectual properly-being. This can embody relaxation techniques, interests, and stress manipulate.

14. Avoid Negative Self-Talk:

Replace terrible self-talk associated with your fitness with high high-quality and increase-orientated language. Encourage your self to take high excellent movement.

15. Learn from Others:

Seek concept and steering from people who've conquer health demanding situations or finished nicely-being goals. Their memories can encourage and inform your journey.

Applying a Growth Mindset for your health and nicely-being journey allow you to overcome barriers, make more healthful options, and hold a effective outlook to your nicely-being. By drawing near these disturbing situations with self-control and a focus on reading and boom, you may gain and keep pinnacle fitness.

Managing Stress and Anxiety with a Growth Mindset

Stress and tension are common demanding situations in life, however a Growth Mindset may be a effective device for managing and overcoming them. Here's a way to conform with a Growth Mindset to deal with pressure and tension effectively:

1. Embrace Stress as a Learning Opportunity:

See pressure as a risk to learn how to manipulate and adapt to tough situations. A Growth Mindset permits you to view stress as a regular part of life which can motive personal growth.

2. Reframe Negative Thoughts:

Challenge horrible and self-defeating mind that make a contribution to strain and anxiety. Replace them with extra great and constructive ideals about your ability to manipulate and find out answers.

three. View Anxiety as a Signal for Growth:

Recognize that tension can be a sign that you're stepping outside of your consolation area. Use it as a motivator to face demanding situations and research new skills.

four. Develop Coping Strategies:

Cultivate wholesome coping mechanisms for managing strain and anxiety. These can also encompass relaxation techniques, mindfulness, meditation, deep breathing carrying sports activities, or physical pastime.

5. Maintain Self-Compassion:

Be kind and compassionate to your self, particularly in a few unspecified time in the future of instances of stress and tension. Avoid harsh self-criticism, and renowned that it's k to war.

Chapter 4: Case Studies And Real-Life Examples

Certainly! Here are some case studies and actual-life examples of individuals and corporations making use of a Growth Mindset to conquer challenges and accumulate fulfillment:

1. Carol Dweck's Research:

Dr. Carol Dweck, a psychologist, is concept for her large research on the Growth Mindset. Her research have confirmed that students who consider in the capability to growth their intelligence thru attempt and analyzing generally tend to outperform human beings with a hard and fast mind-set. Dweck's art work has had a profound effect on education and has recommended the adoption of increase-orientated training strategies.

2. Michael Jordan:

Michael Jordan, regularly seemed as one of the greatest basketball game enthusiasts in statistics, is an example of a Growth Mindset in sports activities activities. He confronted setbacks and screw ups, which incorporates being reduce from his excessive school basketball group. However, his willpower and perception in his capability to decorate led him to a couple of NBA championships and a notably a achievement profession.

three. SpaceX and Elon Musk:

SpaceX, led via manner of Elon Musk, exemplifies a Growth Mindset within the region of place exploration. Despite dealing with severa setbacks and disasters, which encompass rocket explosions, Musk and his institution maintain to investigate from their mistakes and enhance their generation. This increase-orientated approach has enabled SpaceX to emerge as a pacesetter within the aerospace industry.

four. J.K. Rowling:

The creator of the Harry Potter series, J.K. Rowling confronted more than one rejections from publishers in advance than accomplishing fulfillment. Her notion in her writing and her capacity to persist via traumatic conditions is a testomony to the electricity of a Growth Mindset.

5. Microsoft and Bill Gates:

Microsoft's co-founder, Bill Gates, is idea for his resilience and determination to mastering. He dropped out of college however continued to teach himself and construct his employer. Microsoft's success is in component because of Gates' willingness to research from errors and adapt to new annoying situations.

6. Malala Yousafzai:

Malala Yousafzai, a Nobel laureate and recommend for women' education, became centered with the resource of way of the Taliban for her activism. Despite going through existence-threatening challenges, she continues to promote schooling for women worldwide. Her unwavering dedication to her motive exemplifies a Growth Mindset.

7. Khan Academy:

Khan Academy, an internet schooling platform, turn out to be based totally through the usage of Salman Khan with the perception that all people can have a look at and decorate. The platform offers unfastened academic belongings and adaptive gaining knowledge of equipment, promoting a Growth Mindset in training.

eight. Pixar and Ed Catmull:

Ed Catmull, a co-founding father of Pixar, fostered a innovative way of life wherein failure is seen as a natural a part of the modern technique. The company's determination to analyzing from errors has brought about severa successful animated films.

These case studies and examples show off that a Growth Mindset can be applied in severa domain names, which includes education, sports activities, entrepreneurship, and personal development. They spotlight how individuals and agencies can triumph over demanding situations, studies from screw ups, and achieve success with the resource of adopting a attitude that values strive, reading, and resilience.

Personal Stories of Overcoming Obstacles

1. Oprah Winfrey:

Oprah Winfrey grew up in poverty and confronted severa demanding situations, alongside aspect abuse and discrimination. She overcame the ones obstacles to grow to be one of the maximum influential and a success media moguls in the global. Her willpower and notion inside the energy of education and self-improvement led her to exceptional fulfillment.

2. Stephen Hawking:

Renowned physicist Stephen Hawking modified into recognized with a rare shape of motor neuron illness at a younger age. Despite his debilitating situation, he persisted to make groundbreaking contributions to the sector of theoretical physics and authored numerous outstanding-selling books. His story is a testomony to the triumph of the human spirit over bodily boundaries. 3. Malala Yousafzai:

Malala Yousafzai, a Pakistani activist for ladies' training, survived a Taliban assassination try at a more youthful age. She endured her advocacy for ladies' education, turning into the youngest Nobel Prize laureate. Her resilience and unwavering willpower to her purpose have stimulated humans worldwide.

4. Nick Vujicic:

Nick Vujicic became born without limbs, going via severa physical and emotional worrying situations. He has end up a motivational speaker and creator, inspiring human beings together collectively together with his message of preference, perseverance, and self-popularity.

five. Nelson Mandela:

Nelson Mandela spent 27 years in jail for his anti-apartheid activism. Upon his launch, he have become the President of South Africa and a international image of reconciliation and forgiveness. His story is a powerful example of the capability to overcome political and social limitations through resilience and backbone.

6. Bethany Hamilton:

Professional surfer Bethany Hamilton out of place her left arm in a shark attack at the same time as she come to be truely 13 years antique. Despite this lifestyles-changing occasion, she decrease lower back to competitive surfing and have turn out to be an inspirational decide within the worldwide of sports sports activities.

7. Elon Musk:

Elon Musk, the CEO of SpaceX and Tesla, confronted numerous setbacks and economic traumatic conditions in his early career. He even invested his private cash to hold his companies afloat. Musk's relentless pursuit of his imaginative and prescient for the future of vicinity exploration and sustainable power is a story of tenacity and innovation.

8. Amanda Gorman:

Amanda Gorman, the inaugural poet for President Joe Biden's inauguration, overcame a speech impediment to come to be a celebrated poet and public speaker. Her self-control to overcome her demanding conditions and use her voice for amazing change is a superb private tale.

These private testimonies serve as powerful reminders that barriers and adversity can be conquer with resilience, self-control, and a Growth Mindset. They inspire others to bear in mind in their very personal ability to conquer traumatic conditions and advantage their aspirations

Athletes and the Growth Mindset

Many athletes exemplify the mind of a Growth Mindset in their method to sports activities sports and opposition. Here are a few strategies in which athletes include this mind-set:

1. Embracing Challenges:

Athletes with a Growth Mindset see annoying conditions, each in training and opposition, as possibilities to look at and enhance. They welcome difficult combatants and traumatic physical activities as possibilities to emerge as higher.

2. Learning from Setbacks:

Instead of being discouraged through losses or awful performances, athletes with a Growth Mindset view them as possibilities for increase. They have a have a look at their mistakes, make essential changes, and are to be had returned stronger.

three. Resilience:

Athletes regularly face injuries, setbacks, and tough intervals in their careers. Those with a Growth Mindset are more resilient and bounce back from the ones demanding situations with strength of will and a focus on improvement.

four. Effort and Hard Work:

A Growth Mindset encourages athletes to do not forget inside the electricity of attempt and difficult art work. They recognize that fulfillment is a result of strength of mind, exercise, and non-prevent development.

5. Adaptability:

Athletes want to evolve to diverse situations, combatants, and conditions. A Growth Mindset fosters adaptability, permitting athletes to modify their techniques and techniques as wished.

6. Self-Belief:

Athletes with a Growth Mindset have a strong self-notion. They recognise that their abilities can be advanced with try and training, and that they technique worrying situations with self assure.

7. Feedback and Coaching:

Athletes are open to comments from coaches and teammates. They use this feedback as a treasured tool for reinforcing their competencies and normal ordinary overall performance.

8. Goal Setting:

Athletes with a Growth Mindset set smooth and bold goals for themselves. These goals feature motivators and benchmarks for progress.

9. Visualizing Success:

Many athletes use visualization techniques to anticipate themselves succeeding. They don't forget that intellectual training is in truth as critical as bodily schooling.

10. Staying Positive: - A exquisite mind-set is crucial in sports activities. Athletes with a Growth Mindset reputation on their strengths and development, keeping a excessive high-quality outlook even within the face of traumatic situations.

11. Enjoying the Process: - Athletes apprehend that fulfillment isn't pretty masses winning however moreover approximately the delight of the journey and the technique of development. They locate success inside the daily grind of schooling and competing.

12. Motivation thru Adversity: - Adversity may be a powerful motivator for athletes with a Growth Mindset. They use setbacks and troubles as gas to push themselves to new heights.

thirteen. Mentorship and Support: - Many athletes are trying to find mentorship and help from skilled coaches and teammates. They cost steerage from those who can help them boom and enlarge of their sport.

These trends of a Growth Mindset aren't most effective applicable to athletes however also can encourage human beings in severa additives of life. Athletes who embody this mindset often find out themselves not best accomplishing fulfillment of their undertaking however furthermore becoming feature models for the electricity of determination and non-stop improvement.

Acknowledge and have amusing your small victories and achievements alongside the way. These

Entrepreneurs and the Growth Mindset in Business Success

Entrepreneurs who consist of a Growth Mindset are more likely to benefit industrial business enterprise fulfillment. Here's how they comply with this thoughts-set to their endeavors:

1. Embracing Challenges:

Entrepreneurs with a Growth Mindset view worrying conditions as opportunities for innovation and boom. Obstacles do not deter them however as an alternative see them as opportunities to take a look at and beautify their groups.

2. Learning from Failure:

Instead of seeing failure due to the fact the give up of a task, entrepreneurs with a Growth Mindset see it as a precious lesson. They examine what went wrong, adapt their strategies, and are available lower returned stronger.

3. Resilience:

The business company global may be hard, with usaand downs. Entrepreneurs with a Growth Mindset are resilient and get higher from setbacks with a focal point on development and fulfillment.

four. Adapting to Change:

Entrepreneurs need to adapt to converting market conditions, patron alternatives, and generation. A Growth Mindset encourages adaptability and the functionality to pivot at the identical time as important.

five. Belief in Effort and Hard Work:

Entrepreneurs apprehend that fulfillment is a end give up end result of determination, attempt, and non-stop development. They are willing to position inside the art work to benefit their desires.

6. Seeking Feedback and Mentorship:

Entrepreneurs are open to comments from clients, employees, and mentors. They use this feedback to refine their services or products and make informed choices.

7. Setting Ambitious Goals:

A Growth Mindset conjures up entrepreneurs to set formidable and possible dreams. These dreams feature motivators and guideposts for the boom of their agencies.

8. Focus on Innovation:

Entrepreneurs with a Growth Mindset fee innovation and constantly are seeking out new methods to remedy issues and meet the desires in their target audience.

9. Positive Mindset:

Maintaining a exquisite outlook is crucial in entrepreneurship. Entrepreneurs with a Growth Mindset focus on answers, possibilities, and the charge they may be able to provide to customers.

10. Persistence and Grit:

Entrepreneurs are mentioned for their staying power and backbone. A Growth Mindset encourages them to stay devoted to their imaginative and prescient, even though confronted with adversity.

11. Self-Belief:

Entrepreneurs have a strong belief of their talents. They understand that they could growth the abilties had to be successful, and they approach demanding situations with self notion.

12. Learning from Success:

Entrepreneurs do no longer quality take a look at from screw ups; further they examine from their successes. They take a look at what labored nicely and the manner to mirror the ones successes inside the destiny.

13. Goal-Oriented:

Entrepreneurs with a Growth Mindset set specific, measurable, and time-bound desires. These goals help them live focused and tune their development.

14. Adaptability and Innovation:

A Growth Mindset encourages marketers to live bendy and open to new mind and technology. They are inclined to alternate route once they see possibilities for increase.

15. Mentorship and Networking:

Many a hit marketers are searching for mentorship and collect sturdy networks to benefit insights and manual their increase journey.

16. Focus on Customer-Centric Solutions:

Entrepreneurs frequently prioritize providing charge to their clients. They constantly are trying to find to apprehend purchaser desires and adapt their products or services because of this.

17. Celebrating Achievements:

Entrepreneurs famend and have a good time milestones, that would assist preserve motivation and a high excellent employer tradition.

Entrepreneurs who exercise a Growth Mindset to their enterprise ventures are much more likely to navigate the challenges of entrepreneurship, studies from their memories, and in the long run gain sustainable fulfillment. Their belief in the power of try to studying positions them to conform and innovate in a all at once converting industrial corporation panorama.

Students and the Growth Mindset in Academic Achievement

Students who undertake a Growth Mindset commonly generally tend to excel of their instructional hobbies. Here's how they observe this thoughts-set to gather achievement:

1. Embracing Challenges:

Students with a Growth Mindset welcome educational challenges as possibilities to investigate and expand. They are not discouraged by way of difficult subjects or assignments however view them as opportunities to enhance their abilties.

2. Learning from Failure:

Instead of seeing awful grades or mistakes as screw ups, college college students with a Growth Mindset see them as stepping stones to improvement. They have a look at their mistakes, are trying to find remarks, and paintings to accurate them.

3. Resilience:

Academic life can be demanding, with setbacks and disappointments. Students with a Growth Mindset are resilient and get better from instructional traumatic situations with determination and a focus on development.

4. Effort and Hard Work:

A Growth Mindset instills in college university students the perception that educational success is not sincerely decided thru innate capability however by means of the use of attempt and backbone. They apprehend that putting in the paintings is vital.

five. Adaptability:

A Growth Mindset encourages adaptability and the capability to regulate have a look at techniques and strategies as favored. Students are open to new analyzing strategies and techniques.

6. Belief in Learning:

Students with a Growth Mindset have a sturdy notion within the power of mastering. They approach schooling with the understanding that they could broaden new talents and statistics through strive.

7. Goal Setting:

Setting smooth instructional goals and goals motivates university students. These desires feature benchmarks for improvement and help preserve interest and motivation.

eight. Seeking Feedback:

Students actively are searching out remarks from teachers, friends, and mentors to apprehend their areas of development and regulate their observe strategies because of this.

9. Persistence:

A Growth Mindset promotes persistence and grit. Students remain devoted to their educational goals despite the fact that faced with difficult coursework or complicated subjects.

10. Self-Belief: - Students don't forget in their academic talents and apprehend that they are able to amplify the abilties crucial for success.

This self-perception gives them the self assurance to cope with hard topics.

11. Learning from Success: - Students do no longer most effective examine from their errors but furthermore from their successes. They study what they did right and are seeking to copy those a fulfillment strategies in the destiny.

12. Positive Mindset: - Maintaining a outstanding and constructive outlook is key to academic fulfillment. Students with a Growth Mindset reputation on their improvement, getting to know, and the satisfaction of overcoming academic challenges.

thirteen. Adaptation to Change: - As the academic panorama evolves, college college students with a Growth Mindset live adaptable and open to new strategies of studying, in conjunction with technology and possibility educational sources.

14. Mentorship and Support: - Many students trying to find mentorship and academic help

from teachers, tutors, or older university college college students who can offer steering and belief.

15. Celebrating Achievements: - Recognizing and celebrating instructional achievements, irrespective of how small, allows university university college students hold motivation and a immoderate first-rate outlook.

Students who observe a Growth Mindset to their instructional journey are much more likely to navigate annoying situations, analyze from critiques, and ultimately excel in their studies. They apprehend that try and studying are the keys to fulfillment, and they live open to new strategies and techniques to decorate their instructional achievements.

Creative Minds and the Growth Mindset in Innovation

Individuals with present day minds frequently leverage a Growth Mindset to strain innovation. Here's how they exercise this mindset to foster creativity and innovation:

1. Embrace Uncertainty:

Creativity and innovation frequently involve exploring uncharted territory. Those with a Growth Mindset encompass the uncertainty and capability for failure as part of the creative device.

2. Learn from Failure:

Rather than being discouraged with the beneficial aid of progressive setbacks, human beings with a Growth Mindset see them as possibilities to research and decorate their innovative mind. They take a look at what went incorrect and refine their strategies.

three. Resilience:

The modern approach can be difficult and complete of obstacles. A Growth Mindset fosters resilience, permitting humans to bounce back from creative disasters and maintain pursuing revolutionary answers.

four. Belief in Effort and Experimentation:

Creative humans consider within the power of try and experimentation. They recognize that innovation calls for difficult art work, exploration, and a willingness to iterate and refine ideas.

five. Openness to Feedback:

Creative minds actively are searching for comments from friends, mentors, and audiences. They view comments as a precious tool for reinforcing and outstanding-tuning their modern standards.

6. Adaptability and Change:

A Growth Mindset encourages adaptability and the functionality to pivot while crucial. Creative individuals are open to converting their modern techniques and perspectives in reaction to new data and challenges.

7. Goal Setting and Vision:

Setting visionary dreams for innovation motivates revolutionary minds. These goals function guiding standards and inspire human beings to push the boundaries of what's possible.

eight. Self-Belief and Confidence:

Creative human beings keep in mind in their capability to generate new and progressive ideas. They understand that creativity can be superior and honed through the years.

9. Learning from Success:

Creatives do not only examine from their modern missteps however additionally from their successes. They have a look at what worked properly of their revolutionary endeavors and are trying to find for to replicate the ones a achievement factors.

10. Positive Mindset: - Maintaining a exceptional and optimistic attitude is crucial for innovation. Creative people popularity at the capability of their thoughts and the delight of overcoming revolutionary stressful situations.

11. Continuous Learning and Exploration: - A Growth Mindset encourages a self-control to non-stop gaining knowledge of and exploration. Creative people are open to new affects and are inclined to extend their information and skills.

12. Collaboration and Diverse Perspectives: - Creativity often advantages from collaboration and the incorporation of severa viewpoints. Those with a Growth Mindset are open to operating with others to generate innovative answers.

thirteen. Reflection and Iteration: - Creative minds reflect on their paintings and constantly iterate and improve their innovative mind. They recognize that the revolutionary machine is an ongoing adventure.

14. Celebrating Achievements: - Recognizing and celebrating progressive achievements, regardless of how small, enables hold motivation and a pleasant modern tradition.

Creative those who comply with a Growth Mindset to their paintings are more likely to navigate innovative traumatic conditions, research from every successes and disasters, and continuously push the limits of innovation. They view attempt, experimentation, and flexibility as crucial additives of the innovative way.

Lessons from Historical Figures

Historical figures from various fields have furnished treasured education that keep to inspire and guide humans these days. Here are some training we will research from a choice of historic figures:

1. Mahatma Gandhi:

Lesson: The power of nonviolent resistance.

Gandhi's strength of mind to nonviolent civil disobedience introduced about large social and political trade. His existence teaches us that peaceful, persistent activism can result in transformative societal shifts.

2. Leonardo da Vinci:

Lesson: The rate of hobby and interdisciplinary thinking.

Da Vinci's huge-ranging interests, from paintings to technological know-how to engineering, emphasize the importance of being a lifelong learner and the benefits of coming near problems from a couple of angles.

3. Nelson Mandela:

Lesson: The power of forgiveness and reconciliation.

Mandela's capability to forgive and are looking for reconciliation after 27 years in prison helped heal a divided america of the united states and establish a more equitable society in South Africa.

four. Marie Curie:

Lesson: The significance of patience and backbone.

Curie's pioneering paintings in radioactivity and Nobel Prizes exhibit that relentless willpower to at the least one's passions and desires can bring about groundbreaking discoveries.

five. Martin Luther King Jr.:

Lesson: The energy of a dream and collective motion.

King's "I Have a Dream" speech and leadership within the civil rights motion remind us that a compelling vision and collective motion can bring about social justice.

6. Amelia Earhart:

Lesson: The value of courage and breaking gender barriers.

Chapter 5: Cultivating A Growth Mindset In Others

Cultivating a Growth Mindset in others, whether or not it's far your kids, college students, personnel, or pals, may additionally have a profound impact on their private and expert improvement. Here are a few strategies to assist instill a Growth Mindset in others:

1. Model a Growth Mindset:

Lead with the aid of example. Demonstrate a Growth Mindset to your non-public lifestyles with the useful resource of embracing demanding conditions, studying from disasters, and constantly looking for self-development. When others see you valuing boom, they are more likely to comply with in form.

2. Encourage Effort and Persistence:

Praise and recognize tough work, attempt, and perseverance in place of absolutely focusing on outcomes or innate skills.

Highlight the price of attempting, making errors, and attempting once more.

3. Provide Constructive Feedback:

Offer remarks this is specific, positive, and focused on regions for improvement. Encourage people to view remarks as a tool for increase and mastering in desire to as grievance.

4. Foster a Learning Environment:

Create an surroundings wherein errors are seen as possibilities to analyze, and in which human beings enjoy regular to take dangers and find out new mind with out the concern of failure.

five. Promote Goal Setting:

Help others set easy and feasible goals. Encourage them to break large desires into smaller, workable steps. Goal placing offers motivation and a sense of route for increase.

6. Highlight the Power of "Yet":

Teach the concept of "but" with the aid of manner of inclusive of it to statements like "I do no longer recognize this...Yet." This easy word conveys the idea that information and boom are ongoing techniques.

7. Share Success Stories:

Share memories of people who've triumph over obstacles and done achievement thru effort and perseverance. These memories can encourage others to undertake a Growth Mindset.

8. Encourage Self-Reflection:

Encourage human beings to reflect on their strengths and regions for development. Help them set apart time for self-evaluation and purpose making plans.

nine. Promote the Use of "Not Yet" Lists:

Encourage individuals to create lists of capabilities or talents they've got now not mastered however. This can serve as a seen reminder of the capability for increase.

10. Mentor and Support: - Provide steerage and mentorship to help human beings amplify and examine a Growth Mindset. Offer manual in putting and accomplishing goals.

11. Use Positive Reinforcement: - Reinforce Growth Mindset behaviors with super remarks. Let human beings recognize once they showcase developments like try, resilience, and versatility.

12. Offer Challenges: - Present hard duties that push human beings past their comfort zones. Encourage them to see the ones demanding situations as opportunities to develop.

thirteen. Encourage Collaboration: - Promote collaboration and the sharing of mind. Collaborative environments regularly encourage a Growth Mindset as humans studies from every extraordinary.

14. Provide Resources for Learning: - Offer get proper of entry to to sources for expertise

development and growth, including books, guides, workshops, and mentors.

15. Celebrate Achievements: - Acknowledge and feature fun milestones and achievements, regardless of how small. Recognizing progress reinforces the idea that boom is valued and advocated.

Cultivating a Growth Mindset in others is a effective way to foster non-public and expert development. It encourages humans to method worrying conditions with a great mind-set, a willingness to analyze, and the notion that they might decorate their talents over the years. By using these strategies, you may help create a lifestyle of growth and improvement in any surroundings.

Teaching a Growth Mindset to Children

Teaching a Growth Mindset to children is a treasured agency that could set them on a course of lifelong mastering and resilience. Here are a few techniques for instilling a Growth Mindset in children:

1. Praise Effort and Process:

Instead of praising innate abilties or consequences, awareness on praising the attempt, techniques, and tough work that kids positioned into their sports activities activities. Encourage them to look that attempting, making errors, and persisting are all praiseworthy.

2. Teach the Brain is a Muscle:

Explain to kids that the mind is kind of a muscle that could broaden stronger with try and exercise. Share memories and examples of approaches the thoughts develops after they studies new topics.

3. Use the Power of "Yet":

Teach kids to add "but" to their vocabulary. When they say they can't do something, remind them to mention, "I can't do it however." This easy phrase means that boom and reading are ongoing tactics.

4. Discuss Famous Failures:

Share reminiscences of well-known folks that confronted failure and setbacks but ultimately finished incredible achievement. Emphasize that even the maximum completed people had to triumph over worrying conditions.

5. Encourage Goal Setting:

Help kids set practical and potential goals. Break down big desires into smaller, feasible steps. Goal placing offers motivation and a feel of route for increase.

6. Promote a Love of Learning:

Foster a love for gaining knowledge of and interest by using way of encouraging youngsters to find out their pursuits and passions. Support them in pursuing new capabilities and knowledge.

7. Emphasize the Process, Not Just Outcomes:

Shift the focus from achieving the cease end result to appreciating the journey and attempt worried in reaching that end result.

Encourage youngsters to fee the approach of getting to know and growing.

8. Encourage Mistakes and Learning from Them:

Teach youngsters that making mistakes is a natural a part of mastering and growing. Discuss what they could research from their mistakes and the way they'll enhance.

nine. Be a Growth Mindset Role Model:

Demonstrate a Growth Mindset in your very non-public life. Share tales approximately your very own annoying conditions and the way you have triumph over them via analyzing and attempt.

10. Provide Constructive Feedback: - Offer comments this is specific and wonderful. Help children understand what they did properly and the manner they may decorate. Encourage them to appearance comments as a tool for boom.

11. Avoid Labels: - Refrain from labeling children as "smart" or "no longer clever" based on their ordinary performance. Labels can restrict their notion of their functionality to develop and examine.

12. Use Growth Mindset Language: - Encourage youngsters to apply phrases that replicate a Growth Mindset, such as "I'll deliver it my excellent shot" or "I can discover ways to do that."

13. Encourage Self-Reflection: - Teach kids to mirror on their strengths and areas for development. Help them set aside time for self-evaluation and motive making plans.

14. Celebrate Achievements: - Acknowledge and function an first-rate time each small and large milestones and achievements. Recognizing progress reinforces the idea that boom is valued and recommended.

15. Offer Challenges: - Provide kids with tough responsibilities that encourage them to stretch their abilties. Encourage them to view

those demanding situations as possibilities to increase.

Teaching a Growth Mindset to children is an investment of their destiny. By instilling the perception that attempt, studying, and resilience are keys to fulfillment, you help them amplify the attitude and capabilities to overcome demanding conditions and collect their goals.

Promoting Growth Mindset in Educational Settings

Promoting a Growth Mindset in educational settings is crucial for fostering a tradition of studying, resilience, and fulfillment. Here are strategies for educators, instructors, and administrators to inspire a Growth Mindset in schools:

1. Educate Educators:

Ensure that teachers and school team of workers understand the concept of a Growth Mindset and its significance. Provide education and sources to assist them include

Growth Mindset thoughts into their coaching practices.

2. Model a Growth Mindset:

Teachers and college leaders need to guide thru instance. Demonstrate a Growth Mindset for your very very very own getting to know, expert development, and response to challenges.

three. Praise Effort and Process:

Encourage teachers to reward university college students for his or her tough artwork, perseverance, and the strategies they use to treatment issues. Shift the focus from praising innate capabilities to valuing the system of getting to know.

four. Set High Expectations:

Establish excessive but possible academic necessities and expectancies for university college students. Believing in their ability to fulfill these requirements can encourage university students to attempt for excellence.

5. Encourage a Love of Learning:

Foster a love for analyzing with the resource of allowing students to find out their hobbies and passions. Create opportunities for independent studies, creativity, and inquiry-based totally projects.

6. Embrace Mistakes as Learning Opportunities:

Normalize mistakes as a part of the studying technique. Encourage university university students to view errors as opportunities to observe, growth, and enhance.

7. Promote Goal Setting:

Teach college students a manner to set unique, viable desires. Encourage them to break down massive objectives into smaller, potential steps.

eight. Use Growth Mindset Language:

Integrate Growth Mindset language and phrases into the lecture room. Encourage college college students to use terms like "yet" and "I can learn how to do that."

9. Provide Constructive Feedback:

Offer comments this is specific, effective, and targeted on regions for development. Help college college students recognize what they did well and the way they will decorate their skills.

10. Foster a Growth Mindset Culture: - Create an environment wherein a Growth Mindset is a part of the faculty's way of life. Use Growth Mindset posters, bulletin boards, and lecture room shows to reinforce the concept.

11. Encourage Self-Reflection: - Teach students to mirror on their strengths, demanding situations, and areas for development. Help them set aside time for self-evaluation and purpose making plans.

12. Celebrate Achievements: - Acknowledge and have amusing milestones, every small and huge. Recognizing development

reinforces the idea that increase is valued and encouraged.

13. Differentiate Instruction: - Recognize that scholars have diverse learning styles and paces. Provide differentiated steering to residence man or woman desires and resource every student's growth.

14. Provide Opportunities for Autonomy: - Allow college college college students to have a few control over their getting to know technique. Encourage impartial studies and self-directed studying.

15. Promote Collaboration: - Foster a enjoy of collaboration and community inside the study room. Encourage university college students to art work together on tasks, research from each different, and percentage their achievements.

sixteen. Offer Mentorship and Support: - Provide possibilities for university students to are attempting to find mentorship and guidance from instructors, older university students, or network participants who can inspire and guide their growth.

17. Evaluate and Adjust: - Regularly verify the effectiveness of Growth Mindset responsibilities inside the college and make adjustments as needed to make certain they align with the school's mission and scholar dreams.

Promoting a Growth Mindset in educational settings can purpose more engaged, stimulated, and resilient students. By instilling the belief that try, studying, and perseverance are keys to success, educators can assist college students thrive academically and extend capabilities that allows you to benefit them inside the course of their lives.

Fostering a Growth Mindset in the Workplace

Fostering a Growth Mindset in the place of business can bring about expanded worker motivation, innovation, and widespread organizational achievement. Here are strategies for employers and leaders to encourage a Growth Mindset among their personnel:

1. Leadership via Example:

Leaders have to model a Growth Mindset of their non-public artwork and problem-solving. Show a willingness to investigate, adapt, and embody traumatic conditions, setting the tone for the organization.

2. Encourage Risk-Taking:

Create a subculture wherein employees revel in cushty taking calculated risks and attempting new techniques. Reinforce the idea that errors are possibilities for studying and increase.

3. Praise Effort and Learning:

Recognize and praise employees for his or her attempt, resilience, and self-discipline to mastering and development. Acknowledge the journey of private and expert growth.

four. Provide Opportunities for Learning:

Offer get entry to to education, workshops, and assets that permit personnel to collect new skills and knowledge. Support ongoing professional improvement.

5. Promote Goal Setting:

Help personnel set easy, capability dreams and offer ordinary feedback and guidance to tune their development.

6. Celebrate Successes and Milestones:

Acknowledge and feature a laugh individual and group achievements, no matter how small. Reinforce the idea that development and accomplishments are valued.

7. Offer Constructive Feedback:

Provide specific, positive remarks to help personnel apprehend their strengths and regions for development. Encourage them to appearance feedback as a device for boom.

eight. Create a Culture of Continuous Improvement:

Emphasize the significance of everyday improvement in approaches, merchandise, and services. Encourage personnel to are looking for for extra inexperienced and effective strategies of doing matters.

nine. Normalize Learning and Growth Conversations:

Make learning and boom discussions a normal a part of one-on-one meetings and general ordinary performance critiques. Create an surroundings wherein employees feel snug discussing their improvement.

10. Foster Mentorship and Peer Support: - Encourage personnel to are looking for mentorship from skilled colleagues or to shape peer aid companies to percentage information, insights, and extremely good practices.

11. Use Growth Mindset Language: - Integrate Growth Mindset language and phrases into the place of work. Encourage employees to

apply words like "but" and "I can discover ways to try this."

12. Promote Collaboration: - Create opportunities for go-useful collaboration, wherein personnel from precise businesses can art work together to research from each extraordinary and contribute to innovation.

13. Evaluate and Adjust: - Continuously check the effectiveness of Growth Mindset obligations within the place of business and make vital changes to align them with the organisation company's goals and values.

14. Encourage Intrapreneurship: - Support and reward personnel for producing and enforcing new mind in the enterprise. Encourage them to count on creatively and take ownership of their initiatives.

15. Provide Autonomy and Flexibility: - Allow personnel the freedom to find out new thoughts, increase modern solutions, and put into impact modifications in their artwork processes.

sixteen. Recognize the Value of Diversity: - Embrace variety in idea, experience, and history. Recognize that one-of-a-kind views can result in greater innovative answers and increase possibilities.

Fostering a Growth Mindset within the place of work encourages personnel to view worrying situations as possibilities, embody gaining knowledge of and improvement, and come to be extra resilient in the face of exchange. This can result in a extra recommended, modern, and adaptable personnel that drives the organisation's achievement.

Coaching and Mentoring for Growth

Coaching and mentoring are effective gadget for fostering a Growth Mindset in human beings. Whether within the context of personal development, schooling, or the place of job, right right right here are techniques for effective training and mentoring for boom:

1. Establish Trust:

Building a basis of take delivery of as right with is vital. Encourage open and sincere communication to create a secure area for sharing stories, stressful situations, and aspirations.

2. Set Clear Goals:

Work with the man or woman to set clean, precise, and viable goals. These dreams feature benchmarks for boom and provide course for the education or mentoring relationship.

three. Encourage Self-Reflection:

Encourage humans to reflect on their strengths and areas for improvement. Help them understand wherein they presently stand and in which they want to move in their boom journey.

4. Focus on the Process:

Emphasize the importance of the getting to know technique, strive, and non-prevent improvement. Encourage people to apprehend the adventure, no longer certainly the prevent consequences.

five. Promote Self-Awareness:

Help people benefit a deeper information of themselves, their beliefs, and their notion styles. Self-cognizance is a vital element of personal boom.

6. Offer Constructive Feedback:

Provide precise, positive feedback that facilitates humans recognize their strengths and regions for improvement. Encourage them to view feedback as a device for increase.

7. Normalize Mistakes:

Reinforce the concept that making errors is a herbal a part of studying and growth. Teach human beings to take a look at from their errors and disasters.

eight. Use Growth Mindset Language:

Integrate Growth Mindset language into discussions. Encourage the usage of phrases like "however" and "I can discover ways to do that" to decorate the concept of non-stop development.

nine. Celebrate Achievements:

Acknowledge and feature a laugh achievements and milestones, no matter how small. Recognizing improvement reinforces the idea that increase is valued and encouraged.

10. Offer Guidance and Resources: - Provide guidance and endorse assets in conjunction with books, publications, workshops, or additional mentors to aid man or woman growth.

11. Promote Goal Setting: - Help human beings set sensible and formidable dreams that align with their non-public or expert aspirations. Goals feature motivation and a experience of path.

12. Encourage Risk-Taking: - Support human beings in taking calculated risks and stepping out of their consolation zones. Challenge them to include new studies and demanding situations.

thirteen. Foster Adaptability: - Encourage human beings to be open to change and adaptable of their strategies. Growth frequently entails adjusting to new instances and stressful situations.

14. Promote Continuous Learning: - Highlight the charge of ongoing studying and self-improvement. Encourage human beings to are searching for opportunities to boom their knowledge and abilties.

15. Offer Mentorship and Support: - Provide mentorship, steering, and assist to help human beings navigate their growth journey. Share your very private stories and insights as a mentor or teach.

sixteen. Evaluate and Adjust: - Continuously test the effectiveness of the coaching or mentoring dating. Adjust strategies as had to better help the individual's increase.

Coaching and mentoring for boom are powerful processes to assist human beings encompass a Growth Mindset, triumph over annoying situations, and recognize their ability. By supplying assist, steerage, and a extremely good surroundings, you can help individuals increase the notion that effort, studying, and non-stop development are the keys to success.

Building a Growth Mindset Culture in Organizations

Building a Growth Mindset way of life in corporations can cause superior innovation, resilience, and worker engagement. Here are techniques to foster a Growth Mindset inside your corporation:

1. Leadership Commitment:

Ensure that leaders in any respect levels are dedicated to and actively screen a Growth

Mindset. Their movements and phrases set the tone for the whole enterprise.

2. Training and Education:

Provide education and academic packages that assist employees apprehend the concept of a Growth Mindset and how it applies to their artwork.

three. Model a Growth Mindset:

Leaders and executives need to steer by using manner of example, embracing demanding situations and reading opportunities, and demonstrating resilience within the face of setbacks.

4. Align with Organizational Values:

Ensure that Growth Mindset ideas are aligned with the agency's values, venture, and goals. Make it clean that boom and improvement are crucial to success.

5. Promote Risk-Taking:

Encourage employees to take calculated dangers and embrace new demanding situations. Foster a tradition wherein errors are visible as opportunities for getting to know.

6. Encourage Continuous Learning:

Promote ongoing reading and capabilities development. Support personnel in searching for opportunities for boom and education.

7. Provide Regular Feedback:

Offer comments that focuses on growth and improvement. Help employees apprehend their areas for improvement and the manner they could art work to enhance their talents.

8. Set Clear Expectations:

Establish easy expectations for worker popular performance and growth. Make sure personnel recognize the standards for fulfillment.

nine. Celebrate Effort and Learning: - Acknowledge and feature fun hard art work, resilience, and the pursuit of expertise, no longer surely the final results.

10. Embrace Innovation: - Encourage personnel to generate and percent innovative thoughts. Create an surroundings wherein innovative wondering is valued and rewarded.

eleven. Provide Mentorship and Coaching: - Offer mentorship and training to resource personnel in their boom adventure. Pair a top notch deal much less professional employees with mentors who can provide guidance and concept.

12. Foster a Learning Culture: - Create a manner of existence of non-forestall learning, in which employees are recommended to find out their pastimes, are trying to find new demanding situations, and increase new talents.

thirteen. Use Growth Mindset Language: - Integrate Growth Mindset language into the employer commercial enterprise organisation's verbal exchange. Encourage employees to apply phrases like "but" and "I can learn how to do this."

14. Encourage Inclusivity: - Embrace variety of belief, experience, and records, as exceptional perspectives can bring about extra revolutionary solutions and boom opportunities.

15. Promote Cross-Functional Collaboration: - Create opportunities for personnel from remarkable departments to collaborate and percentage information and opinions.

sixteen. Measure and Recognize Growth: - Develop overall performance metrics and popularity packages that emphasize growth, development, and development alongside conventional measures of achievement.

17. Evaluate and Adjust: - Continuously look at the effectiveness of Growth Mindset obligations within the commercial enterprise organisation. Be willing to modify techniques as had to align with the agency's goals and values.

Building a Growth Mindset lifestyle in organizations calls for a concerted try from management, a dedication to studying and development, and a focus on fostering resilience and innovation When employees include the concept that strive, analyzing, and non-save you improvement are valued and advocated, agencies can thrive and adapt to change greater effectively.

Chapter 6: What's Mindset?

The mind is a totally effective tool and it in the end determines who you're as someone. Also known as thoughts-set, this questioning sample or your frame of mind influences how you are making feel of the sector in addition to of yourself.

So in unique phrases, a mind-set is a set of ideals and thoughts that have an effect at the manner you cope with any given scenario. It pretty plenty dictates your individual assisting you type out what's taking area round you and what you need to do about it.

How Mindsets Are Formed

Since time immemorial, human beings have idea, acted and fared in any other case from each different. For the maximum aspect, not unusual experience dictates that those differences rise up from the variances in a unmarried's background, studying tales and training Plus, studies additionally elements within the equal course.

So whilst research, backgrounds and education are all outside variables, even internal variables like genetic make-up have a detail to play.

Most experts today agree that forming a mind-set is a mixture of the two. For instance, whilst truely each person comes with a totally precise set of genetics, their testimonies, training and private efforts take them the relaxation of the manner.

So your existence reports and genetics together assist frame your thoughts-set and ideals. And for the reason that every have an critical element to play to your mind-set, it lets in to apprehend what the ones factors are all approximately.

First off, your mind-set to a few component is the manner you placed or sense approximately it, specially at the equal time because it shows within the manner you behave.

Your thoughts-set may additionally need to have taken into consideration one in every of a type additives including an emotional element or how a few aspect or someone makes you enjoy. Then there is the cognitive factor that's how or what you consider the undertaking. This is ultimately located via the behavioral element which indicates the manner you behave while confronted through using the state of affairs.

Then there are your ideals which are merely feelings of truth about a few detail. Beliefs are based totally definitely mostly on mind and at the same time as at a specific thing, the ones mind begin to experience fantastic, they trade into ideals. Beliefs, in turn form your mindset which in flip shape your thoughts-set.

Attitudes and beliefs then offer upward push to habits which may be an immediate mirrored photograph of your mindset.

Perhaps the most common and broadly recognized example of a mindset is seeing the glass as "half of empty" or "half of complete".

Types Of Mindsets

There are specific types of mindsets that would every assist you unharness your super or incorporate your ability. There will be an prolonged list of those but right here are some which have been sponsored by way of way of the use of research. Here's a brief examine the following:

Abundance Mindset vs Scarcity Mindset

The way you view abundance or shortage in certainly one of a kind factors of life significantly affects your achievement in existence, For instance, bear in mind that people are on foot down the street. They are talking to every different, laughing, joking and all the on the identical time as breathing in and respiration out.

Now do you located that one of the can also fear that there may not be enough oxygen for the every of them? Likely not, considering air is sufficient.

Now location the same people scuba diving wherein one's tank starts to malfunction. That man or woman signs the want for oxygen and abruptly the air round them turns into a precious commodity.

This scarcity ought to with out issues make the 2 worry with a hassle that what if there isn't enough oxygen for the every of them?

For the most element, the general population appears to be extra inclined towards a lack mentality. They regularly view existence as having best masses and inside the occasion that they had to share, there wouldn't be sufficient for them.

This unhappy mentality makes it very hard for such humans to percent something together with credit score rating, reputation, duty or possibly authority with others. Instead they first-rate turn out to be competing for to be had belongings despite the fact that there may be an abundance of them.

On the opportunity hand, human beings with an abundance mentality are not restricted via this thinking pattern. Instead of seeing possibility as constrained, they are attempting to create more opportunity for themselves and consist of exchange in choice to fearing it.

To sum up, a person with a lack thoughts-set chooses horrible mind and adopts a sufferer mentality. At nice, their normal attention is on all the topics that may not be jogging.

But others with an abundance mind-set usually will be inclined to place all their energy reserves into what is running and observe limitless opportunities to decorate their cutting-edge-day scenario.

Productive Mindset vs Defensive Mindset

This combination essentially deals with regular overall performance. Many human beings may think that they've a inexperienced mind-set or that they may be being efficient, whereas they'll be truely definitely being busy; in fact, they may not be productively completing obligations and finishing duties.

Think about your each day to-do list and the ten or so assets you need to get finished with the aid of manner of the give up of the day. You might also moreover have spent all your day running round and 'doing' stuff however even as it's 5 pm and also you wrap up for the day, you recognize that you simplest controlled to tick off three of the 10 stuff you have been presupposed to do. You experience consisting of you're operating all the time but don't actually get a bargain done.

Does this imply that you're lazy and don't want to collect your desires? Or in all likelihood it has some thing to do together collectively together with your attitude.

Having a powerful thoughts-set technique which you make use of all of your assets which include some time, strength and efforts within the excellent possible way. At the equal time it moreover approach which you don't try to do the whole lot, be anywhere or perhaps do it within the quickest way possible.

Quite the other, it way making the maximum of what is available on the equal time as taking detail in the technique. Those with a efficient mindset trying to find out valid knowledge that is testable and use their reasoning to make knowledgeable alternatives.

As such, the ones people find out a manner and spend more time finding answers to higher overall performance in desire to finding issues and getting caught.

Chapter 7: Why Is Mindset Important?

Now every mindset cans paintings in a dual way. For instance, on the equal time as your man or woman mind-set can open doorways for you, it could additionally set severe obstacles based in your beliefs and technique in particular scenarios.

This way that surely as mindsets can help you spot opportunities, they could similarly well trap you in self-defeating cycles as properly. The tales which you tell yourself and the matters that you believe about your self can pass either manner.

First off, if you become trapped in a terrible or limiting thoughts-set then your attitude will prevent change from happening in your life. But in case you expand a effective attitude then you allow new abilities to blossom.

Importance Of Mindset In Life

Because your mindset holds your set of beliefs, it has good sized capacity to make a difference in your life. For most humans their beliefs are the middle in their efforts. As such, ideals distinguish parents which might be a fulfillment at what they do in preference to others who continuously battle.

These beliefs form the premise of wherein your abilties come from. Just think about your abilties, your intelligence, and your character. Do you keep in mind those developments to be truly fixed and eternal, or do you found those are elements which you may domesticate and enhance on via lifestyles?

The stress or flexibility approximately those beliefs is what determines your attitude.

Having the proper mind-set for any precise mission is sort of a prerequisite for fulfillment. Whether you're a determine, teacher, student, entrepreneur, or in every other profession, you need the right attitude to acquire fulfillment at what you do.

Every career comes with its very non-public hurdles and barriers and having a effective mind-set lets in you to no longer handiest conquer those boundaries however even welcome them as demanding situations or an possibility to analyze and make bigger.

If you go searching you, you'll see that frequently people with comparable occasions have very unique effects in lifestyles. This occurs due to their mind-set.

Since your thoughts-set regarding activities and conditions influences your interpretation of them, the effects might be wonderful from someone else with a brilliant mind-set.

If you've had been given a remarkable attitude, you'll discover it less complicated to triumph over setbacks than others with a bad or limiting attitude. Or, when you have a terrible mind-set, you'll sense the arena crumble below your ft every time there can be an ugly revel in.

If your middle ideals don't help you, then you definately simply'll possibly set your self up for failure whilst faced with a hard scenario.

You may be more at risk of surrendering and admitting failure on the equal time as all you want to do is try extra difficult or probably address a great technique. You may also need to alternate your frame of thoughts.

Mindsets Are More Than Beliefs

But mindsets aren't mere ideals and characteristic the capacity to dictate your reactions to situations and different dispositions. They serve some of cognitive abilities and assist you to body conditions. At the equal time, your thoughts-set might also even direct your interest to the most critical cues and clear out beside the point information so that you don't overwhelm your self.

Your mindset may additionally offer you with direction through recommending practical dreams to gather so you have a revel in of path. Once your mind-set will become everyday, it defines who you're and what you can grow to be.

Life Experiences Reinforce The Mindset

For the bulk of people, their attitude is created for them at an early age. It may be via parents, teachers, buddies or others which you quite truly absorb what you're suggested.

And because of the fact at the same time as you're younger and haven't any different component of reference, you are taking delivery of the provided understanding. This easy records then becomes embedded internal your psyche and starts offevolved to shape your ideals about the sector and your vicinity inside it.

As you increase and mature, existence studies and activities can also contradict that in advance expertise and actually change your mind-set. However, the sooner know-how maintains to stick and turns into your reference issue for much of your existence. For instance, if you're surrounded via oldsters which is probably in a ordinary america of america of anxiety and weigh down then there's an top notch risk which you'll broaden a thoughts-set that mirrors reactions to life in methods which might be traumatic and crushed.

Your attitude continues developing and will become more potent the greater you repeat and workout your ideals.

Now in case you grow to be locked in a awful or proscribing thoughts-set, then you definately actually'll probably keep repeating horrible self-communicate and begin to see matters in a certain way. This exercise can become self-exciting till you in reality take into account it to be proper.

On the opportunity quit of the spectrum, when you have a notable mind-set then it receives reinforced via your beliefs and consequent movements.

The Emotion Factor

However, repetition isn't the handiest issue at play inside the introduction of conduct and beliefs. The emotion thing additionally plays on this equation. When you blend repeated thoughts and moves with feelings, the anticipated effects can regulate.

Both helpful and lousy conduct get created the same way- through repetition. But the dependancy may be embedded extra quick and strongly whilst blended with emotion.

Take the example of comfort eating. You recognise that it's no longer right for you however as it makes you enjoy suitable at a time while you are down, you switch to this dependancy to elevate up your spirits. Once you get into this cycle, you growth a conduct paired with powerful emotion and an dangerous consuming dependancy is formed.

What Does Science Say About Mindsets?

Neuroscience or the have a have a look at of the concerned tool tells us that the mind is typically developing and destroying neural pathways. These pathways, in turn, form our thoughts and conduct patterns which tell your brain to make picks, select out moves and gift you to the outdoor international.

Among the ones, the pathways which might be used more grow to be stronger, at the equal time as others that stay underused grow to be willing and in the long run be replaced.

This clinical statistics correlates with the purpose of numerous mindsets due to the truth the mind is prewired with the prejudice to investigate new matters. At the identical time, there are also the ones folks that discover ways to prevent getting to know and turn out to be trapped in a tough and fast thoughts-set.

People with nice mindsets are more likely to enhance which complements the idea that potential may be better. On the flip facet, people with a bad mindset appear to stagnate which complements the idea that they get caught at their contemporary-day capacity stage and not the use of a development.

These precise are of hassle to us on this e-book and are referred to as the boom mind-set and the regular thoughts-set. The distinction some of the is that on the same time as one specializes within the effects completed, the opportunity stresses on the method.

The constant mind-set prioritizes outcomes which incorporates getting "that machine" or losing "those 30 pounds" in which the person thinks that they will be described thru the give up result. The boom mindset tells you that the strive placed into the way of conducting that stop end result is more critical.

This is because you can come to be greater clever, more contemporary, and additional a success via focusing at the way and now not the final consequences. It leaves loads of room for development which means you continue to develop as someone.

Going ahead, permit's take a better observe every kind.

Chapter 8: Fixed Vs Growth Mindset

By now you recognize that the way you remember your potential has a completely actual impact at the results you benefit in life. Interestingly enough, both constant and growth mindsets are distinctly self-reinforcing, however in vastly exceptional techniques.

If you don't forget that potential is an ingrained or fixed characteristic that you were born with and might't trade, then you definately own a hard and speedy thoughts-set. But in case you suppose that you can expand this capability thru try and exercising then you definately virtually have a boom mind-set.

Each perception consequences specially behaviors and consequently precise results Of the 2, having a boom mind-set, in that you're organized and inclined to examine and enhance, is the vital factor to achievement.

Having said that, it doesn't recommend that difficult paintings, staying electricity and battle aren't vital They are, but simplest while you agree with which you aren't constrained and are in entire manage of your future.

Mindset In Practice

Individuals with these mindsets no longer high-quality expect otherwise but additionally react to records in a considered one of a type manner. In reality, the variations may be stark after they respond to records approximately wellknown overall performance.

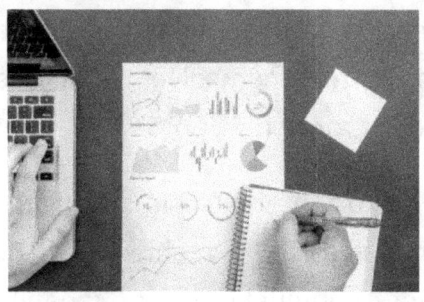

For example, people with a tough and fast mind-set reply thoroughly to statistics about how properly they've got accomplished a few element. It can be something from trying out a cutting-edge recipe, getting to know a new language, running on a DIY project, or doing nicely on take a look at effects and grades. Their minds are most energetic once they look at their suitable ordinary performance. Their top, but rather restrained undertaking is with the results accomplished with strain on the praise they gather.

On the alternative hand, people with a growth thoughts-set have a tendency to be maximum responsive at the same time as they may be informed approximately the approaches they may enhance their normal performance. These oldsters want to learn how to better themselves which leaves a whole lot of room for boom.

They are extra interested in strategies to help them evolve and the technique of doing so, now not genuinely their capabilities or capacity.

The are, in truth very one-of-a-kind techniques, with the preceding being targeted on "How did I do?" in choice to the latter which gives with "What can I do better subsequent time?"

The regular mind-set is all approximately how the performance come to be perceived and the growth mindset is about how improvement can take place. It isn't hard to see which mindset will yield better results in the long run.

Mindset In Action

When it includes taking motion, each the regular as well as the boom mind-set are also poles aside. To test with a very well-known example, permit's take the story of the tortoise and the hare.

In the tale, the hare modified into so excellent that he have to win that he sat down and went to sleep at a few degree in the race. On the opportunity hand, the tortoise grow to be chronic and saved going believing that that he had a hazard of triumphing.

When the hare woke up, he started out walking as rapid as he must however he turn out to be truely too past due. In the interim, the tortoise had obtained.

So the story indicates that the hare had a tough and speedy mind-set wherein he believed that his inherent capability for tempo would in all likelihood guarantee a win. But the tortoise confirmed a increase attitude wherein he believed he needed to art work hard to get to a certain element. At the equal time, he changed into now not frightened of failure however geared up to deal with a project.

This also factors out to the truth that a set thoughts-set can be susceptible to a very excellent completed view of oneself. Much similar to the hare, this questioning sample suggests that you are already best. And so your mind becomes less adept at recognizing opportunities for development.

The Basics of Fixed vs Growth Mindset

People with a set thoughts-set take transport of their developments as a given. They receive as true with there may be a sure quantity of intelligence and abilities and there can be not a few factor that would change this truth. So human beings with this thoughts-set are regularly concerned about their developments and the way good enough they may be.

With a hard and fast mind-set you believe that your functionality is innate and you find out failure unsettling because it makes you question how well you simply are. Another perception shared via way of humans with this mind-set is that there's a hidden pinnacle restriction to what you can attain.

For example, if you've struggled via college, you can well accept as true with that you're now not reduce out for university. You may also in no way even attempt out for university but get caught in a low paying, non-attractive interest as a substitute. Such a hobby obtained't do a little element for stimulating your thoughts and the belief of inadequacy will become your fact.

On the opportunity hand, when you have a growth attitude, then you definitely clearly accumulate that you could enhance your ability and failure exceptional tells what you need to art work on.

Those who have a difficult and rapid mindset are all about proving themselves and often turn out to be shielding want to everybody factor out that they made an mistakes. This thoughts-set only permits human beings to degree themselves by using the usage of the usage of their failures.

The growth attitude, however frequently well-knownshows resilience and perseverance in the face of mistakes. Instead of adopting a shielding technique, they grow to be triggered to better their general overall performance.

Take a have a have a examine those u.S.A. Of mind statements with the useful aid of human beings with a set and growth mind-set:

Fixed thoughts-set Growth mind-set

I'm terrible at math. Math has been hard for me.

I can't seemtoget prepared. I've attempted my hand at organisation, but with out loads success.

I love cake, but I can't bake. I'd want to have a look at baking, but I haven't started out however.

I'm no authentic at origami. I haven't learnt the way to do origami yet.

It's smooth to look from those examples that rates from the constant mind-set organisation are extra of a declaration of resignation inclusive of "terrible at", "can't appear to", "can't bake" and "no correct at". There's an implied unwillingness to attempt because the man or woman believes that the ones abilties are past their scope. A enjoy of finality prevails interior this enterprise business enterprise.

The increase thoughts-set organization gives examples which may be extra of an assertion than a assertion. These evaluations mirror that there is the possibility of learning a ability if the person places in some more try and attempts extra hard.

So at the same time as distinguishing the fixed thoughts-set from the boom thoughts-set, preserve the subsequent in mind:

Goals: The fixed mind-set wants to appearance smart while the increase mindset desires to research and enhance.

Challenge looking for: The constant mindset avoids demanding situations but the increase thoughts-set seeks it out.

Change: Change is seen as a danger by means of way of using the consistent mind-set but the increase mind-set perspectives similar to a task.

Response to setbacks: People trapped in a difficult and rapid thoughts-set respond poorly to setbacks, appearing helpless however those with a increase thoughts-set appear resilient.

Chapter 9: The Dangers Of A Fixed Mindset

The blessings of a boom mindset may additionally additionally seem apparent, but many humans have a tough and fast mindset in powerful conditions. This can be very counterproductive because of the truth this mind-set prevents vital skills from developing and developing. This, in turn sabotages your happiness and fitness within the future.

As an example, allow's assume which you aren't a technological statistics whiz. If you preserve telling yourself which you aren't a technology person or that generation isn't your detail, then that statement turns into an excuse to not have a have a look at era.

While with a difficult and rapid mind-set, you could keep away from brief term failure, you also are hindering your capability to expand, take a look at and acquire new abilities in the long run.

On the opportunity hand, your peer with a increase thoughts-set tries to offer technological information a go but failing inside the starting. Now this character probably sees failure as a sign to keep operating on their capabilities in choice to accepting that they aren't actual at a few element.

In the long time, your peer will optimize their capability as they selected to advantage from criticism rather than ignoring it. They decided to triumph over a challenge as opposed to avoiding it and spot it as a mastering opportunity in place of feeling threatened.

So if you count on such things as "It's now not viable to lose the burden", "I'm no longer a herbal artist", "I'm no longer innovative", or "I'm a procrastinator" then you definately'll pass over out on many opinions. In the cease, you finish, don't examine as a awesome deal and it will become decidedly greater difficult to get any better.

Here are one-of-a-type components you'll pass over out on:

Undermining The Importance Of Effort

In a hard and fast thoughts-set, primary characteristics, which incorporates talent or intelligence are taken into consideration regular developments. Such people have a tendency to report their expertise or intelligence in preference to enlarge them. They might also additionally moreover credit rating competencies on my own to achievement, without effort. When they may be specific at a few detail, they gladly characteristic it to their competencies collectively with scoring excessive on a test or doing properly on a challenge. However, at the identical time, moreover they don't forget their shakier abilties to be steady as properly. So in choice to developing those competencies they may be predisposed to in fact be given them as is with out a attempt invested on development, inclusive of "I'm now not lessen out to address a paint brush".

They get keep of that they may be the way they'll be and may't get any better at it or trade.

The Obsession To Prove Worth

People with a tough and speedy attitude experience a want to show their worth. Every state of affairs needs a affirmation of their person, intelligence, or person.

Every state of affairs is also overly evaluated ensuing in questions like "Will I prevail or fail?", "Will I appearance dumb or smart?", "Will I be rejected or commonplace?" and so on.

Although they appear determined for approval, they aren't going to transport past their capabilities to attain the achievement they need so badly. They commonly have a tendency to get stuck because they're afraid of being rejected that they're not willing to expand beyond their shell.

The Desire To Be Flawless

Taking it a step further, the hassle with a hard and fast mindset is that it isn't sufficient definitely to achieve success neither is it enough to appearance smart and gifted. If some thing, the selection is to seem pretty an awful lot ideal.

So what takes vicinity in the long run is that if failure method you lack capability or competence, then you definitely are stuck being a failure. There is nowhere to move from this problem.

Instead you come to be specializing in fending off failure at any price and try and maintain feelings of fulfillment. You don't attempt a few element new due to the fact in case you don't expect you'll excel at it, you don't want others to look you fail. In the surrender, the complete method can be very limiting and tense.

Decreasing Self-Knowledge

Perhaps one of the most negative results of a fixed mind-set is that it decreases self-know-how. Instead the focal point shifts to outside rewards and validations. With this mind-set, hobby is taken away from internal development.

By continuously striving for outdoor popularity and signs and signs and symptoms of fulfillment, you normally have a tendency to deceive not simplest others however yourself as nicely. It additionally takes faraway from who you truly are.

The Need for Constant Validation

Your mind-set also can impact your dating with others. Often humans with a fixed thoughts-set revel in insecure and anticipate their partners, friends, buddies and others to assist them in each state of affairs.

They simplest need to be spherical folks who reward them for his or her competencies and supply them self assurance they had been unable to establish for themselves. However, this will gift problems for what if the romantic liaisons quit, friendships fall out or battle arises amongst peers?

Any of those conditions would go away someone with a hard and rapid mind-set with low esteem, terrible self perception and a whole lot of doubt and fear.

To summarize, right right here is how a hard and fast mindset appears at matters: Skills: The fixed mind-set believes that is something you're born with which could't be modified.

Challenges: The constant attitude regards this as a few aspect to keep away from in any respect charges. There is the everyday hazard that a undertaking have to display your lack of expertise and you usually tend to surrender with out troubles whilst in such role.

Effort: This is taken into consideration useless with the aid of the usage of the regular thoughts. It's a few thing that people hotel to when they aren't precise sufficient for the technique.

Feedback: Feedback makes the fixed attitude get on the protecting. When given feedback, human beings with this mind-set take it in my view and consider it an specific attack on their overall overall performance or talents. If it isn't to their liking they will even forget about approximately the comments absolutely.

Setbacks: When confronted with setbacks, humans with a difficult and fast attitude will placed the blame on others. They also get discouraged effortlessly and are more likely to give up certainly.

Remember that the ones are all triggers that not handiest establish but moreover deliver away a tough and rapid thoughts-set.

Switching from one to the alternative may be tough but is viable. You need to take a look at out for the ones triggers because of the fact a hard and rapid mind-set can and will keep you again. Specific behaviors to transport a long way from a tough and fast thoughts-set can encompass the subsequent guidelines:

Listen to your internal voice- in case you don't reap this, it will rule your behavior in a recurring manner, retaining you stuck in that you are.

When you find out someone higher than you, studies from them.

When you're confronted with a preference amongst something steady and some thing hard, move for the project.

When you hit a bump in the road, ask your self what you could research from it or what you can do next.

When you bought remarks, don't get angry or take it as private grievance. Think of methods how you can use these facts to higher your overall overall performance.

Chapter 10: The Power Of A Growth Mindset

A boom mind-set permits people to view themselves as able to doing properly in maximum, if now not all settings. They definitely don't undergo in thoughts themselves as restrained with the aid of manner of their modern skills, but believe that they're capable of do a little factor they want as long as they practice.

Consider the instance of being given a brand new undertaking, a few problem which you haven't worked on earlier than. Now your response needs to pass each way.

You have to observe this new assignment and expect that you're not licensed to do those paintings or that such numbers, techs or designs weren't your cup of tea. This might manifestly mirror a set mind-set and you'd omit out on the whole lot stated within the preceding financial ruin.

However, you could also take a look at the identical and start making plans how you could make it artwork. You have to deliberate what you'd need to maintain to the table and what it'd take to get the favored results. This optimism and creativity advise a growth thoughts-set on the way to additionally empower you to gain the subsequent:

Improvement Through Effort

A increase thoughts-set allows humans to accept as real with that their number one competencies can boom through difficult paintings and self-control. For this lot, brains and capabilities are clearly the start factors and allow them to assemble on the ones.

This institution of humans well-known a fervour for getting to know and resilience that could be a must for accomplishment. People with a increase mind-set view their abilties as tendencies which can be superior through their willpower and attempt.

Being of a increase attitude you're inclined to strive out new subjects due to the truth your fulfillment is based upon in your attempt and not any innate capacity. You're not centered on fending off failure due to the fact you recall that if you do poorly you may enhance and reach time. Plus research additionally suggests that boom attitude permits people to navigate strain and stressful conditions better and bring about higher degrees of well-being.

Offers A Sense Of Fulfilment

Unlike the fixed thoughts-set, one of the maximum obvious benefits of the boom thoughts-set are the limitless possibilities to be availed. With a boom mind-set, you always pursue betterment accompanied with the aid of way of a sense of success and fulfilment.

A experience of success is also a precursor to a higher state-of-the-art of excellence. In the approach you observe that achievement is a continuous art work in development in area of immediately gratification.

Develops Resilience

A boom mindset also lets you amplify resilience. When you face demanding situations or setback, your mind-set takes a more extraordinary technique coping with those.

For example, at the same time as you're given feedback, you realize that it's an effective mastering method to help you set appropriate dreams and requirements for the future.

Buffers Against Demotivation

People with a increase mind-set are looking for for out opportunities and demanding situations to interact them in choice to get their satisfaction from consequences. This manner being stimulated to do increasingly.

Being extra method oriented, in desire to in simple terms stop end result orientated, the ones human beings thrive while they're within the manner of doing something. The gadget offers a reading possibility, stimulates them and drives them on to do even extra.

As an example, in preference to wishing for a completed e-book, written perfectly, the growth attitude is motivated to show up each day to paintings on it constantly till it is completed, no matter what it takes. Instead of being fixated on pretty quite a number on the scale, a increase attitude will popularity extra on working out every day to become extra match and wholesome.

Encourages Perseverance

A increase attitude moreover needs perseverance. The attention of a increase attitude isn't to concentrate on what occurs to you however on what takes area for you.

Perseverance additionally technique kicking fear of failure out the door. This portions to taking possibilities even as possibility affords them and not restriction your self to residing a totally cautious or paranoid lifestyles.

Tenacity is an crucial detail for a growth mindset. And because of the reality you could't continuously have a 100% fulfillment rate with each venture you address, tenacity will help mirror to your failures inside the right way.

Failure to discover a solution normally opens up an possibility an remarkable manner to art work in your abilties and research something new. When most humans hit a wall, they both make an excuse or simply surrender. However, someone with a growth thoughts-set realizes that failure is an inevitable element of assignment achievement.

As such they put together for failure mentally, understanding that it's going to come at some time or the alternative. The concept neither scares them nor makes them surrender.

Plus, permitting your self to fail a touch takes the pressure off of getting an fantastic give up give up end result each time.

Promotes Critical Thinking

When you speak approximately mastering, making mistakes is a have to because it forces you to understand in which you made a mistake. This attempt also permits you no longer satisfactory pinpoint an answer however additionally develop critical wondering.

Let's expect you get a specially intricate question in magnificence. Should you switch off your thoughts because of the truth you sense overwhelmed, you'll in no way increase or examine a few issue.

However, if you renowned the trouble by way of manner of jogging it relentlessly, asking questions and evaluating considerably, you have got a better chance of finding a solution. At the identical time, the strive which you put in will help your mind create new neural connections and grow to be higher ready at fixing comparable problems. That's the way you develop and be higher at anything.

Practice Makes Perfect

Not to overuse an age vintage cliché, but for a boom mind-set practice does indeed make high-quality, or greater successfully masses higher at what you workout.

Since the increase mind-set is introduced on more by using manner of a power of thoughts for learning in preference to a craving for approval, workout and strive promote developments like creativity and intelligence. Individuals with this mindset neither get discouraged through failure, nor do they recall themselves as failing however as learning.

In truth, training over and over does have a good sized position within the getting to know way and is vital to attaining records. One detail that most experts agree on is that schooling improves common overall performance and adjustments the thoughts.

To summarize, a increase attitude sees the following conditions as: Skills: The increase mindset believes that capabilities are a few trouble that you may continuously alternate, enhance and growth. Skills come from difficult work so you can't stop walking.

Challenges: The growth mind-set is eager to encompass demanding conditions and views them as an possibility to broaden. The chance to engage in a undertaking makes the boom mind more continual.

Effort: Effort is vital for a growth attitude and might even override know-how. When the boom mind-set sees strive due to the fact the direction to achievement, it realizes the want for lifelong getting to know.

Feedback: The growth mind-set views remarks as a few detail optimistic and an experience to take a look at from. It is an effective means to discover regions that want improvement.

Setbacks: Instead of putting a damper on subjects, setbacks are visible as strategies to decorate on cutting-edge talents and efforts.

Chapter 11: Can You Change Your Mindset?

Beliefs may be modified when they not serve you or will can help you get to your desires.

Resistant To Change

Although mindsets can alternate, this best takes area very slowly. This is in particular right when you have lengthy held beliefs about some factor. For instance, when you have been knowledgeable that consuming an apple an afternoon is ideal for you, you may find it difficult to believe if someone informed you otherwise.

Even even though a hard and fast mind-set is simple to shape, it's miles evidence in opposition to change. Take the example of a stake preserving a tent in its region in the ground. Although it can be moved, once it's been located, you're reluctant to transport it till there is right cause to acquire this. So as soon as you have got have been given long-hooked up a mind-set about some aspect, it situations your destiny opinion approximately that detail. For example, if you do not forget an upcoming occasion dull because of the fact the ultimate one of the same type changed into truely uninteresting you can not want to move in any respect. However, in case you do bypass and discover it to be now not boring the least bit, it may take you some time to alternate your mind-set.

Using Fear To Change Your Mindset

An man or woman with a difficult and fast mindset is extra keen in searching smart than to fail even as learning new things. They will do the entirety they may be capable of to avoid embarrassment and forget approximately what they certainly lack of. In exclusive phrases, they emerge as frightened of looking silly.

This in itself is an inhibiting component. It's a opportunity that this stems from a experience of rejection or ridicule from childhood evaluations or sports stored to your subconscious mind that you can no longer even hold in thoughts consciously.

As a result of this subconscious fear, your regular mind-set avoids attempting new matters, resists getting to know, stalls your improvement and can even make you act lazy.

To counter this successfully and alternate your mind-set, you want to emerge as aware of the concern the usage of your behavior. And then apprehend that this worry has no foundation on your gift reality. You need to overcome it and allow it circulate.

As an instance, students with a set mind-set view their intelligence diploma as unchanging. Their high hassle stays proving that they're clever, or hiding that they're now not.

As such, they typically tend to keep away from situations in which they may fail. They additionally don't get higher properly from setbacks and best pick carrying out obligations that they may already do well.

The identical moreover shows in others with this thoughts-set wherein they limit themselves and sabotage their efforts.

Using Actions To Change Your Mindset

Another technique to converting mindsets is thru moves for the purpose that skills and skills get developed through repetition and consistent exercising. The key to changing a set attitude is identifying and refuting the regular mind-set voice and taking boom orientated movement over and over.

Although this isn't some thing that takes region in a single day, you may extend new skills thru planned and repeated workout. And for every new expertise that you expand, your regular attitude voice weakens.

Identifying Your Counter Mindsets

Mindsets get formed through preceding critiques and emotional milestones. But when the ones mindsets do not supply the consequences you expect, they emerge as counter mindsets.

This effects in generating emotions of self-doubt, limiting beliefs and other terrible mind that get within the way of improvement. For the maximum detail, those horrific thoughts rise up so regularly which you can't additionally be aware about them.

Think about that nudging voice which makes disparaging feedback even as you look inside the reflect. It is the equal voice which makes you sad with the manner you appearance, makes you hesitate at the identical time as coming close to someone new or maybe at the same time as you need to recollect a career exchange.

Now anyone research poor thoughts, or counter mindsets to a unique diploma, but the damage is collateral. It lets in you to habitually damage your desires and makes it very hard to stay first rate. The most effective element that remains are nasty reminders like

"I can't talk to him/her", "I'm no longer clever sufficient for that", "I'm no longer licensed enough" or "I'm out of form" and so on.

To exchange your thoughts-set, you want to be aware about at the equal time as this voice get raised and the manner often it takes place. This will assist you to pinpoint the triggers of you counter thoughts-set and narrow it down to three key subjects.

Shifting Gears From The Negative To The Positive

Once you have were given hooked up your bad thoughts you want to save you them from maintaining you decrease once more. Whenever a poor perception surfaces, counter it via way of giving a direct, but remarkable reaction.

Say you want to transport for a walk after dinner to get in more exercising. But the hassle is that once dinner is over, you start listening to that voice that you're too worn-out, too complete, or that it's too overdue to go out now.

Put a stop to that thinking sample right away thru approach of having up and putting in your walking shoes.

You will find that frequently truely taking that first step is enough to show off that nasty voice in your head.

Understand "WHY" You Need To Change

Changing thoughts-set requires loads of energy of will and tough art work as original conduct aren't smooth to interrupt. This will become even extra difficult for the reason that some of the terrible or proscribing conduct got shaped while you have got been little and you've got been doing subjects the equal manner ever whilst you don't forget that.

Understanding why you want to change a addiction or mind-set will make it greater significant. Here matters need to are to be had handymotivation and energy of thoughts.

First, you'll want to depend upon motivation to get you through changing your behavior, and whilst the "why" will offer you with motivation, it is able to be difficult to maintain in the end. This is in which energy of thoughts need to step in and hold you going.

However, electricity of will can run out pretty quickly too. Think approximately seeking to eat extra healthy and then you definitely definitely find out a % of Girl Scout cookies next to the fruit bowl at paintings. Maybe you get your electricity of mind together and withstand the cookies.

Next, you endorse on going to the gym after paintings however want to stay behind for a few reason. By the time you're finished, you're no longer most effective worn-out however out of strength of thoughts as well. Plus, the reality that you weren't capable of maintain on with your unique plan doesn't assist both.

So do you turn out to be going to the gym or without delay domestic? You in all likelihood apprehend the solution because it takes place to simply all of us.

So while you try and change your behavior thru counting on motivation and self-discipline by myself, those might not be sufficient on their very own. And that's moreover why such a number of humans give up on converting their conduct speedy when they start, not capable of conform with through.

Instead what you want to do is to turn out to be a chunk forgiving and permit your self some region to allowance for mistakes stumble. A steady attitude leaves no

leaving you emotionally tired and hesitant to attempt some thing new.

Start Small To Finish Big

One of the first-rate strategies to change mindsets is to begin small towards large dreams. Trying to become healthy, rich or clever at the thing of extra compassionate, calmer and a success is in no manner smooth.

Once all another time you want to fight all of your demons embedded for your mindset from those early years.

So if you discover yourself burdened maximum of the time, try to meditate for two minutes each night time in advance than sitting in a lotus feature for a right away 1/2 hour and a racing thoughts.

If you would like to become more wholesome, begin with some issue as small as one push up only. Build your electricity up along side your mind-set earlier than you get to an fantastic set of twenty.

Decide on your tiny cause and pursue it with a nice thoughts-set. Oftentimes, you could discover which you in reality do more then what you aimed for (possibly to 3 push u.S.A.In region of 1) and could sense terrific as you over gather. On unique days you can only advantage the minimum but nonetheless revel in top due to the fact you met the cause. Many human beings assume that it's unnecessary to start so small however typically hitting small desires correctly can help shape new mind-set behavior.

Chapter 12: Strategies To Develop A Growth Mindset

When you permit consequences which include your take a look at scores, your weight, your gadget or your appearance outline you, you switch out to be the sufferer of a hard and fast mindset. On the alternative, a growth thoughts-set is all about analyzing and you can accelerate the approach via following a few tried and real strategies.

Continual Learning

A boom mindset is crucial approximately evolving and growing. As such, in preference to attempting to find approval from others, you need to surround yourself with individuals who will let you beautify.

This method that you don't sense forced to justify everything you do. Doing so only manner you sacrifice your functionality for increase. Instead prioritize your studying over approval as this will assist you expand and achieve your ventures.

At the same time, trying new matters will help you offer you with particular thoughts and make you privy to what you are correct at. You can also start hard yourself with new responsibilities to growth your ability.

Be Committed

When you pair chronic mastering with strength of will, you positioned your self up for excellence.

Too regularly people make the mistake of wobbly determination, thinking that they're committed to their cause or aim, but they're virtually not. With a shaky thoughts-set, human beings were given right all the way down to strive subjects after which truly wait to look what occurs.

During the technique many humans satisfactory hobby at the truth that they haven't yet completed their aim and might't prevent thinking about how heaps in addition they want to drift. This limiting mind-set can sabotage your efforts making you extra liable to giving up.

However, at the same time as you expand a boom thoughts-set, this problem gets eliminated. When making a decision that you are absolutely committed to carrying out your goals, no matter any setbacks, you're more likely to succeed.

Here'saverysimple, everydayexample. Youwake up overdue, soar off the bed, already harassed that you will skip over your bus or your vehicle pool. In the frenzy, you skip breakfast, get dressed hurriedly and rush out the door fantastic to find out that you have indeed not noted your journey. Now a hard and rapid mind-set will possibly respond with the beneficial useful resource of muttering, cursing, calling names and live in a awful temper for the relaxation of the day.

But in case you are working within the course of growing a boom, you could see this as an possibility to decide to a extra timely recurring to ensure that this doesn't appear over again.

You will then reply through going to bed early, setting an alarm and laying out your garments within the night in order that the following day is higher and precise.

Don't simply determine to planning it out in your head, but decide to carrying it out in motion.

Develop Healthy Self Esteem

It can come to be very hard to purpose for or obtain achievement with out selfesteem. Before you may preference to increase or improve, you want to believe that you are capable of undertaking your purpose. Since you can't give you the cash for to undermine yourself, it turns into essential which you save you annoying about what others anticipate.

Your conceitedness is the way you observe yourself, a reflected photo of your thoughts-set. It is created from an internal speak with yourself in which you recognize and compare your truly virtually worth whether or not wonderful or bad.

To have a strong conceitedness, you want a strong mind-set, one which allows you to broaden and evolve.

Work On Your Perspective

Every attitude has to do with attitude. Your foundational beliefs, thoughts, biases and attitudes all affect the manner you method statistics and enjoy the sector round you. Having a growth mind-set will increase the danger of formulating a winning angle and conducting long term achievement.

Perspective is also the using pressure inside the returned of motivation. Motivation determines whether or not or now not or now not you're able to attain your set dreams in longterm. It serves as a gasoline to maintain you going till you reap the surrender line. Without motivation, you could lose the energy while faced with troubles. The satisfactory way to maintain your motivation burning is to don't forget your 'WHY' – Why did you start? Why is it critical to you?

For example, at the same time as you want to lose a few weight, is it because of the reality you don't much like the manner you enjoy on your contemporary america or is it due to the fact you truely need to be healthy? While either purpose will pass you toward your intention, the simplest brought on with the resource of using feeling of lack will probable be greater tenuous.

Set Effective Goals

There are many elements which have an effect on an individual's growth mind-set. One among those is placing effective and massive goals.

When goals are set realistically, it becomes greater probably to attain them. Achieving important goals or maybe smaller milestones in the path of a bigger purpose is a extremely good analyzing approach for the boom mind-set.

A thoughts this is resilient gets you thru the hard instances and assist you flow into on to the following task.

Manage Your Inner Negative Voice

One of the maximum important boundaries to having a boom mind-set is your inner essential voice. This voice maintains telling you that you could't do it, it's now not properly really well worth it, you're who you are and also you need to discover ways to stay with that.

This internal voice reinforces the concept that matters are given and you've extremely good were given loads have an effect on over your existence. Everyone, even human beings with a increase mind-set have this voice and to alternate your attitude you need to learn how to manage it.

As an area to start turn the "can't" on your thoughts into "can" and add a "but" to the prevent of you sentences.

Facing Adversity

A growth attitude is a hit in going through adversity. If you need to get thru the hard patches, you'll want to face each project head on.

If you avoid going through obstacles, you may't desire to maximize your modern-day capacity or increase new competencies. Challenges gift an possibility to have a look at and amplify which means that that you can also increase inside the device.

People with a increase mind-set excel at stressful conditions as the ones propel them in advance.

Be Open To Feedback

A growth thoughts-set normally welcomes feedback as it's far every different threat to check. Feedback additionally offers the possibility to enhance your overall performance. It permits making a decision which regions you need to improve and wherein you're doing well.

And when you consider that remarks is supplied with the aid of others, it's very important to interact with different humans. Interacting or networking may include stepping from your consolation location an awesome manner to encourage creativity.

Imagine reaching your workplace wherein your boss calls you in to bitch about a report you've prepared or a project you're coping with. With a hard and rapid thoughts-set, you'll see this as a threat to triumph over your self up. You might also emerge as feeling which you're now not accurate enough for this manner or that your boss is absolute clueless as to what it takes to get the interest performed.

In both case, the relaxation of your day is spent cribbing and complaining and in worst case situations, even hobby searching. But at the same time as you try to extend a increase mind-set you'll see this identical incident as a few detail of a gaining knowledge of revel in. You'll be greater willing to assess your performance and are trying to find powerful feedback that absolutely permits you parent out a way to decorate your challenge. Instead of muttering and mumbling, shifting on may be lots a whole lot less complex.

Chapter 13: Dealing With Setbacks

After debating the best and the bad approximately exceptional mindsets, it will become clearer that the way the thoughts responds to setbacks, disappointments or failure can be very important.

For example, for a difficult and fast mindset a setback turns into a failure that distorts truth. This distorted view prevents people from seeing a scenario for what it's far. And without a clean photograph of the situation, it is able to grow to be no longer viable to pivot, solve or make any improvement.

But for a growth thoughts-set, this setback doesn't become overwhelming. In truth, it's miles frequently seen as a few aspects that permit you to redirect your efforts inside the proper direction.

The Importance of Failure

For the move-getters, failure provides the opportunity to understand the gaps among what they wanted and the effects they have been given.

For everybody interested by enhancing their performance and consequences within the destiny, a hint setback can take them an extended way beforehand. This is due to the fact the setback offers the danger to find out the purpose of the error and then adapt future efforts as a result.

Since it is crucial to understand that there will by no means be a state of affairs in which everything is good, it's far in addition crucial to assume setbacks at the way.

The increase mind-set sees failure as a stepping stone from which it could study the following valuable existence education:

Experience And Knowledge

The first critical lesson learnt from a mistake, setback, or failure is revel in. When you are making a mistake, you are taking with you firsthand enjoy which allows you expand a deeper knowledge.

The enjoy allows you adjust your frame of mind and mirror on the actual nature of factors.

Another problem of the identical is that it brings with it firsthand know-how. If you have increase mind-set, you may use that statistics inside the future to overcome that very identical failure.

Resilience And Growth

Setbacks also assist collect resilience. To come to be a achievement it's far crucial which you comprehend how to be resilient, simply so your first instinct isn't to give up.

The same resilience moreover leads to boom in that you learn how to evolve in the face of adversity. Accepting that it's okay to enjoy an occasional setback allows you to get over failure faster.

Having stated that don't forget at the same time as it's okay to fail, it's now not okay to surrender.

Change Your Strategy

Failure is an effective way to recognise the need for trade on your plans or techniques. While it is important to have an amazing plan in thoughts for success, it must now not be set in stone.

Instead it should be bendy sufficient to let you evaluate your method, adjusting and measuring matters as you flow into alongside. The vital attention in this hassle is that your dreams want to live the same but your plan need to constantly evolve.

Seeking Inspiration through Others

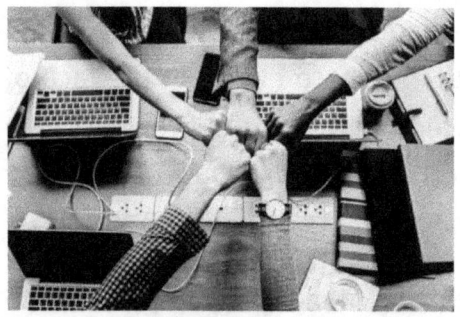

As you have got already seen, the growth mindset seeks idea via others who are higher at something, more a hit and get the popular results.

You may additionally moreover start seeking to famous personalities from all walks of existence and recognize that every a achievement person has lengthy beyond thru some of setbacks earlier than reaching success.

Using Failure As Leverage

You can use any setback as leverage to now not terrific get over however additionally to propel ahead. To leverage your setbacks, you need to recognise what you failed at and why. You additionally want to be aware about what you could do in another manner and a way to avoid the equal mistakes once more.

This mind-set will help you pass past your errors in area of equating failure with whole defeat. With the right mind-set you discover ways to amplify and mature, gain new expertise and mindset on everything from love, life, business agency, coins, relationships and those.

During this method, you're pressured to make new connections and bridge gaps in which you hadn't connected the dots in advance than.

Redefining Priorities And Values

Depending for your mind-set, setbacks can each make you or ruin you. For the growth thoughts-set, failure helps you discovered once more your priorities.

Once you recognise that a setback is simplest a quick hurdle, you discover ways to look beyond it. You start anew reordering subjects which might be most important and shuffle others round. In an try to get better and decorate yourself, you begin to make the wanted changes. At the equal time, each subsequent failure additionally lets in reshape values. Since the growth thoughts-set facilities on constant evolution and improvement, you'll recognize that what you valued ten years in advance than isn't always what you price in recent times.

It's a constant paintings in improvement that learns to move beforehand leaving setbacks within the lower back of.

Don't Let Your Failure Define You

When you come across a setback, it's tempting to allow it form the manner you word yourself. For example, a failed dating can also make you accept as true with which you're not asattractiveasyou idea. Ora jobyou definitely favored however didn't get, must make you get hold of as right with that you're now not that smart however the whole lot.

However, it's essential to apprehend that your nicely truly worth isn't determined thru condition. A higher preference might be to assess your competencies and strengths thru thinking about primary setbacks from the past.

Reviewing the way you overcame those earlier boundaries can help devise a solid approach.

Helps Reach Your Potential

For most people, failing approach that they really attempted. They positioned forth effort to perform a little element profitable which didn't training session. But each trying and failing can emerge as treasured teachers for everybody with a boom mind-set. Failure promotes higher questioning and prepares you to maximize your potential for destiny efforts.

The identical moreover builds you up in approaches you in no way concept viable thru allowing you to take duty in your mistakes. Often instances, it's difficult to realise what you're capable of until you push via failures. This additionally allows in developing your potential.

Failure Is Always Better Than Regret

Failing is a miles better opportunity to regretting. Think approximately living with regret now not knowing what have to've took place had you performed for that job. And then test it with failing to strong the venture but locating out wherein your shortcomings lay. At least with the failure choice you're in the direction of having it proper the following time.

Success that comes clean often go away masses of room for failure because it makes you revel in that not some thing must bypass wrong. But failure allows you no longer underestimate achievement and strive more difficult subsequent time. Regret, on the other hand, presents no such possibility and only leaves you feeling dismal.

Setbacks Yield A Sense Of Direction

Most people hold second guessing the selections they take. They achieve this no longer due to the fact those choices are right or wrong but best because of the truth they aren't certain how things moderate pan out.

But ought to a preference hit a setback, it factors to a course for redirection. Now a growth mind-set is short to grab this possibility and learns from its errors. It develops a experience of readability on wherein topics went incorrect and the manner to redirect your efforts to correct the error.

And because redirection takes you into new venues, you get to discover extra options and step from your comfort sector. In this sense, failure can also help you take away the concern of stepping out of your comfort zone.

www.ingramcontent.com/pod-product-compliance
Lightning Source LLC
Chambersburg PA
CBHW071442080526
44587CB00014B/1950